THE REAL YOU

Leading Your Life From Your Authentic Self

by

Gavin Frye, MA, MFT

First Edition

The Real You: Leading Your Life From Your Authentic Self

Written by Gavin Frye

Published by Authenticity Press

Los Angeles, California

ISBN 978-1-7349790-8-4

The Real You is dedicated to the breathtaking grandeur of the Authentic Self, which resides within each and every one of us.

It is also dedicated to my beloved father, Robert William Frye. Throughout his life he blessed all he encountered with his radiant love, the vibrancy of his physical touch, and his unbridled gratitude for the gift of life.

CONTENTS

Section Two

PATHWAYS TO A DEEPER CONNECTION WITH OUR AUTHENTIC SELF

SECTION ONE

Embracing Authentic Living: A New Paradigm

INTRODUCTION

"I look at you all, see the love there that's sleeping, while my guitar gently weeps. I don't know why nobody told you how to unfold your love"

~ George Harrison

THE INNER LIGHT

Throughout my childhood, whenever I was in the company of adults, I felt compelled to look into their eyes to see if they were shining. Although I rarely encountered adults whose eyes were vibrantly alive, whenever I did, the radiance they were transmitting took my breath away.

For as long as I can remember, I've had a burning curiosity about how these unique individuals kept their Light shining when most other adults' eyes were dull and lifeless. In my early teens, I began mustering the courage to ask them. I, an innocent adolescent, would peer as deeply into their eyes as politeness would allow and say, "Excuse me, I can't help but notice how bright your eyes are. Can you tell me how you keep your Light shining?" They would almost always smile at me. They were never bewildered by my question and knew exactly what I was talking about. They would begin sharing with me the deeper qualities of life they had discovered that were important to them. They often talked about love, about kindness and giving, about family and relationships. I heard stories of forgiveness, summoning the courage to be true to themselves, and their lifelong passion for learning. During these conversations, I had the distinct impression that something essential was being gifted to me. Thus was born my life's dedication: to live as one of those people whose inner Light continued to shine.

BIG QUESTIONS

What is this Light within, and where does it come from? How do some rare individuals find a way to maintain their connection with their inner lighthouse, and how does that bond seem to so easily slip through the grasp of the large majority of others?

I've discovered that each and every person living on this planet, no matter the traumatic experiences they may have walked through, has a unique and natural Self—an eternal presence—that longs to be known, breathed into and lived from. This pure part of us, the core of our nature, can never be harmed or broken—it is always whole and more readily accessible than most people imagine. It's an inner dimension characterized by love, wisdom and compassion. It's astonishingly alive and is a sacred gift each one of us has been granted. We see it clearly in the eyes of very young children, where it is so evident that each of us is born as an utterly unique being of Light.

This is the real you—your Authentic Self.

WE ARE ALL CARRIERS OF LIGHT

Although each of us has an Authentic Self, also known as the Soul, the majority of adults are, for the most part, unaware of its presence and gifts. Most of us lose our connection to this deeper nature within us as we grow up and begin reckoning with the impact of traumatic experiences of one kind or another. Somewhere along life's path, we often mistakenly identify with a very limited story and experience of who we are. We then create a mask for our own protection, and hide behind it, mistakenly believing we really are this false self we project out into the world.

The underlying nature of this planet is that of a school, a fierce school centered around learning, healing and Self-discovery. The "Soul's curriculum" we each have been given isn't easy, in large part because we live in a world that often reinforces mediocrity and fosters a sense of being lost. Few are raised with an orientation toward the awake and empowered world of the Authentic Self, the Light within us.

In grade school through college, the one-size-fits-all educational process has the impact of distancing us from our passion for learning and creativity—core hallmarks of the Authentic Self. The nature of modern schooling is focused on the regurgitation of memorized information with little or no encouragement for spontaneous innovation. For many, this educational system promotes an orientation towards compliance with an outside authority, often reinforcing a sense of disempowerment and passivity. For some, it breeds an attitude of disinterest and, for others, rebellion.

In the midst of this limiting programming, fueled by those around us who are also not living dynamic lives, we can increasingly lose touch with who we really are. Separation from the Authentic Self, which is a major source of anxiety, is a planetary epidemic. Most people are unconsciously ensnared in a negative view of life and a sense of themselves as being small and powerless.

Yet, life has the exciting potential to be lived as a hero's journey of overcoming challenges as we make our way back home to knowing and embracing our deeper Self. You truly can use the difficulties you encounter in life as catalysts to awaken to your true nature, and this book will assist you in that process.

Throughout human history, in the face of enormous opposition, there have been leaders like Marie Curie, Abraham Lincoln, Maya Angelou, Martin Luther King Jr. and others who have made exemplary contributions to society that have inspired successive generations. In order to do so, they had to build a conscious bridge back to their inner core, enabling them to share their Light and gifts with the world. As you are reading this book or listening to it, you may carry a desire in your heart to actualize this profound potential in yourself. What more exciting and meaningful way is there to live?

AUTHENTICITY & THE LIGHT

Each of us instinctively recognizes authenticity when we encounter it in others. We may not be able to describe it in words, but a deeper part of ourselves knows truth when we see it, hear it, and feel it. Authentic presence and expression is often what makes artists and leaders of all kinds well known and beloved. They have gotten a hold of themselves and their unique gifts, and are courageous enough to share their authenticity with the rest of the world.

Unfortunately, in today's world there is a mistaken notion that some people are gifted and some are not. This is simply not true. The reality is that not only are all of us equally worthy, but each of us possesses a unique constellation of genius and calling that is essential for the healing of our culture. This includes you. Maybe your mind has told you otherwise. Maybe people in your life have told you otherwise. They were wrong.

THE RIVER OF LIGHT

In my early 20's, I had a life-changing dream in which I was walking through a forest. I heard the sound of a river roaring up ahead. As I moved through a dense stand of trees toward the melody of the rushing water, a flowing river of pure shimmering Light came into view. It was incandescent gold. It was a powerful and glorious sight. As I got closer, I recognized that my spiritual teacher at the time was standing in the middle of the river. He was looking directly at me and beckoning me to join him in the healing flow of water. As I got still closer, my teacher gently pointed upstream, and as my eyes gazed in that direction, I saw that his teacher was also standing in the middle of the river.

At that moment, the silent underlying revelation I received was that this river was not about my teacher, or even his teacher. Rather, it was a flow of sacred, healing Light that lived within all of humanity. Filled with the realization that our deepest nature is divine Light, I gracefully strode into the river, immersing myself in the shimmering gold.

I've been standing in the healing energy of that river ever since, and have been privileged to assist many others to embrace their own river of Light, which is their Authentic Self. I'm now beckoning you to join me in this river, to take the place that is awaiting you. After all, this sacred river is your birthright.

THE PURPOSE OF THIS BOOK

The Real You is a catalyst, and is being offered as a voyage, an adventure into the great mystery of who you are and why you are here. It is designed to activate your curiosity and desire to cultivate a life-changing relationship with your Authentic Self.

I've approached this book as an intimate sharing of my own life journey, interwoven with a wealth of core insights and life-enhancing tools discovered during my 40 years as a licensed psychotherapist and leadership mentor. My sincere hope is that this book will ignite in you a passion for becoming more alive. As you awaken new creative impulses, you will witness your unique gifts and genius unfolding. I want to support you in gently turning toward yourself in an honorable way—with an orientation of love, curiosity and discovery—and ask inwardly, "*Who* is in here?"

To support you in harvesting the most from this book, I strongly recommend you obtain a personal journal and use it specifically for capturing and reflecting upon your insights and discoveries as you are reading. You might consider calling it your *Authentic Self Journal*.

MY PATH OF TRANSPARENCY

The pioneering psychologist, Carl Rogers, once said, "What is most personal is, at the same time, the most universal." With this in mind, woven throughout this book are my own deeply personal stories. You will get to know me intimately, not just as a detached author or philosophical narrator, but as a man, a human being with joys and triumphs—as well as challenges, flaws and wounds. It is my intention that through the transparent sharing of my life's trajectory you will have insights about your own life's journey.

You will meet my ordinary yet astonishing parents, who bravely traversed many challenges throughout their lives. You will meet my older sister, who became a heroin addict for almost 20 years before turning her life around. You will get to know my older brother, who was a convicted murderer and white supremacist gang leader during his 15 years in prison before he finally peeled off the layers of hatred and homicidal rage and became reacquainted with his Authentic Self. I still marvel at the arc of his life, at the majestic contribution he made to the world after he put down his knives and guns and racism.

Continuing to deepen a relationship with my Authentic Self throughout my life has enabled me to heal and glean the learning from my turbulent teen years when my sister and brother walked their dark paths and our family was decimated in their wake. The deep love and wisdom of my true nature assisted me in overcoming untold suffering later in life as I navigated my own family's challenges with mental illness and drug addiction and the ending of a 25-year marriage. I have moved through many sacred passages of trauma and loss, all of which contributed to me boldly manifesting my most cherished aspirations.

What are your lifelong dreams that you have yet to fulfill? After reading these pages and letting your heart absorb their essence, may you find inspiration and make use of the practical tools and exercises that are offered to help you overcome whatever obstacles have previously prevented you from achieving your goals.

May you never again be defeated by misfortune. You truly can transform your relationship with adversity, heal and strengthen your close relationships, and successfully birth your heartfelt dreams into this world. My sincere prayer is that you bring your relationship with your Authentic Self front and center, and allow it to weave its vibrant presence into your life in ways you can't imagine.

A HIGHER PERSPECTIVE

Why is this book needed right now? Because all sustainable transformational change in the history of our planet has flowed from individuals and groups acting from the indomitable energies of the Authentic Self. Around the world, the escalating environmental, economic, political and public health crises are together reinforcing a sense of powerlessness and despondency at a time when the wisdom, joy and creativity of our deeper nature is needed more urgently than ever before.

Throughout the world there are political, corporate, religious and educational leaders who are operating from old paradigms, leading from the energies of the false self and wielding "power over" versus "power with" others. This short-term gain for ego and greed imperils our global environment and sustained existence.

Over the last decade, it's been spectacular to witness the groundbreaking progress of the LGBTQ, Black Lives Matter, #MeToo and other human rights movements sweeping through countries around the world. These have coincided with the immense fear and loss flowing from the worldwide COVID pandemic, along with the Russia/Ukraine crisis and its polarizing themes of democracy and authoritarianism.

Fueled by the authentic expression of courageous individuals stepping forward, it is profoundly moving to behold people breaking free from shackles that have oppressed those on the planet for thousands of years. As larger and larger numbers of people step forward in their authenticity and let those in power know that we are no longer going to support destructive, authoritative, short-sighted and self-centered leadership, this growing movement cannot be stopped. The fundamental realization that everyone on the planet is worthy and noble in their own right has always been what's driven true evolutionary social change.

You can contribute to this historic time of global transformation by recognizing and owning the grandeur that you carry inside, and by living a braver and more fulfilling life. Strengthening the connection with the power of your inner Light, your love, is the first and foremost contribution you can make to the world at this pivotal moment in history. We're talking about moving beyond the power of the personality or false self into the inspiring and healing energies that flow from your Authentic Self. This book is about coming home, about embracing both your human and Divine heritage.

CHAPTER 1

Trauma & the Birth of Our False Self

"Trauma can also be the body's response to a long sequence of smaller wounds. It can be a response to anything that it experiences as too much, too soon, or too fast. The body's imperative is to protect itself. Period."

~ Resmaa Menakem

The Authentic Self is a Divine river, a mysterious yet at the same time ordinary consciousness that resides in a distinctly different dimension from that of the everyday mind. It cannot be defined in words, so it's important not to get caught in the trap of trying to mentally define the Authentic Self. The key is to discover rich ways to access the *direct experience* of its presence and energetic flow.

STAGES OF AUTHENTICITY

As human beings, we progress through a universal pattern in our lives that mythologist Joseph Campbell referred to as the "Hero's Journey." This journey takes place in 3 distinct developmental stages.

During the initial years of our life we are anchored in *unconscious authenticity*. We live in the moment and effortlessly respond to our natural impulses without thought or self-censorship.

This often idyllic early childhood stage is typically followed by a challenging extended period in which our protective responses to traumatic life circumstances move us into *unconscious inauthenticity*. In this stage, we are motivated less by our natural inclinations than by the desire to protect ourselves, win approval or rebel against authority.

The final stage of the Hero's Journey is when we consciously reconnect with the presence of our Authentic Self and begin embracing the lifelong art and craft of *conscious authenticity*.

THE CALM BEFORE THE STORM

My very first memory occurred around the age of 2. My mom was bathing me in the warm water that filled our kitchen sink. I remember the smell of freshly baked chocolate chip cookies as my father arrived home from work carrying a bag of them from the bakery. As he walked in the door, I can still see the glowing radiance of love emanating from his eyes as they caught mine. It was more delicious than the aroma of the cookies. I was his precious little miracle of a son and I knew from that point forward that he unabashedly adored me.

I grew up in an ordinary home in the San Fernando Valley in Los Angeles, California. Our family was lower middle class and my mom stayed home to take care of us kids. I was the youngest of 3 children. My half-sister, Cathy, was 7 years older than me, and my half-brother, Michael, was 5 years older. They had a different biological father.

My dad, Robert William Frye, taught me a lot about being genuine. He hailed from Wisconsin and was good-natured and unpretentious. His mind did not dominate his personality, which I always found refreshing. He was a devoted father who cherished my mom and loved us kids. He was a real salt-of-the-earth man.

Whenever we walked down the street and passed someone, even if they were complete strangers, my dad would look into their eyes and greet them with a warm hello. Most people did not do this where I grew up. As a result, I've found that I've greeted strangers in this same way throughout my life.

My dad was an auto mechanic. I have fond memories of helping him work on cars in the driveway and taking adventurous road trips together. He had raced cars and motorcycles for much of his life and loved driving, a passion he passed along to me.

My mom, Joan Frye, was tender-hearted and dedicated to supporting us kids in any way she could. Whenever I needed help with my homework or support with my creative projects, she was always right there by my side.

My friends and I loved making handmade paper boats whenever it rained. We set them next to the curb in the fast-moving water that flowed down the street. Running alongside our boats, we laughed together while getting completely soaked. The first boat to reach the end of the street won the race.

In my early years, my mom didn't allow me to cross the street alone. On my 7th birthday, she finally acquiesced to my long-held desire to go 5 blocks in every direction all by myself. I taped a clipboard with a blank piece of paper onto the handlebars of my bicycle, and I'll never forget carefully sketching a growing map of my new world, street-by-street, which magically expanded 5-fold that day.

School life was great. I began calling square dancing classes in the 6th grade, and fell in love with the game of baseball. I soon became a star pitcher in Little League. Overall, I was doing remarkably well. Hank, my collie companion, was always by my side. As a 10-year-old, I thought my life would go on like this forever. Little did I know that everything was about to change…

THE STORM ARRIVES

I was 11. I was watching my brother, Michael, who was then 16, shoot down sparrows from trees with his BB gun. Often, with a strange grin on his face, he would stomp them with his boot as they fluttered, barely alive on the ground, which horrified me. There was a darkness inside my brother—I was afraid of him.

HEROIN

When I was 12, I was helping my dad work on my older sister's '56 Ford station wagon in our driveway. The wheels had been removed and the car was up on jacks. My sister, Cathy, now 19 years old, suddenly appeared at the end of the driveway and ran toward us with a wild look on her face, screaming, "Are those brakes done yet? I've got to have the car NOW!"

My father calmly said, "No, they're not. I need another hour to finish."

"I need the car NOW," she yelled at him. She recklessly jumped into the car, turned on the ignition and put it into gear. As she pressed on the gas pedal, the engine revved loudly and the rear wheel drums spun on their axles.

My dad said, "Stop, Cathy! This is dangerous. The car could fall off the jacks and someone could get killed."

She climbed out of the car in a heroin-induced rage. This wasn't new behavior, as by this time she had been an addict for 2 years and no longer lived at home. She ran wildly into the kitchen, where she proceeded to yank plates and glasses down from all the shelves and throw them onto the floor. I heard them shattering as I followed my dad into the house. Cathy seemed intent on destroying the kitchen just because he hadn't finished the brakes yet. My mom and I watched in horror as my dad tried to restrain her, tears running down his cheeks, begging her, "Cathy, stop! Please stop!"

My heart was breaking as I watched my gentle father, who would never hurt anyone, desperately trying to keep her from hurting herself or us. She clawed at him to get away, and breaking free, ran out of the house and down the street yelling at the top of her voice. Standing in that kitchen and witnessing this scene unfold, my life seemed surreal. What was once our peaceful home had turned into a war zone.

THE STORM BUILDS

Two years later, when I was 14, my 19-year-old brother, Michael, kidnapped a couple at gunpoint and was sent to prison. While he was incarcerated, my parents received a report from the prison graphically describing a stabbing he had committed against an African American fellow prisoner. Within a few years, Michael became one of the leaders of the Aryan Brotherhood, a white supremacist gang that extends into the prison system.

When I was 16, shortly after he was once again released from prison, Michael swept into the house one afternoon with 3 of his friends. I was sitting at our dining room table doing my homework, and was the only one home. They hurriedly began pulling rifles down out of the attic. I had no idea there were guns hidden in the house, and found out later that my parents hadn't either. I was shocked and terrified. One by one, my brother and his friends laid the rifles down on the dining room table right in front of me. They discussed plans for an ambush with the intent to kill. The targets were, once again, African Americans. Michael glanced over at me with an eerie look and smile on his face as he and his friends loaded shiny new bullets into the rifles. I was horrified as this scene unfolded, but also felt paralyzed about what to do because this was my brother and I was afraid of him.

THE FALLOUT

As a result of the trauma surrounding my brother and sister's destructive choices, a disturbing inner shadow gathered strength inside me. Deluged by my own pain, I moved into fight, flight or freeze survival mode which distanced me from my feelings. An unconscious cycle began of storing up painful feelings, then being emotionally triggered and having meltdowns. Reckoning with this pattern, seeded in trauma, became a central part of my life journey.

Around this time I was playing ping-pong with a friend in our garage. After losing a few points in a row, I pounded the edge of the wooden table with my paddle in frustration and began swearing loudly. My next door neighbor yelled out at me from her bathroom, "You can't cuss like that."

I responded by throwing the wooden paddle at her. It crashed through the window where she was standing, terrifying her. She marched right over to talk with my folks.

I pretended to myself and others that I was doing just fine, while in reality, tremendous anxiety, grief and fear were brewing inside me. I did everything I could to not be a burden to my parents, whom I loved dearly. I was also afraid that, like my brother and sister, if I wasn't careful my life would go over the edge as theirs had. I got excellent grades, but often found myself feeling overwhelmed and agitated.

Around the same time, I was pitching in a Little League baseball game. When the umpire began called my pitches "balls" that I thought were actually strikes, I lost it. I yelled and cursed at him at the top of my lungs. I was promptly thrown out of the game, and as I walked back to the dugout in front of my team and the large crowd, I felt embarrassed and ashamed. I didn't know what was happening to me. I began distancing myself from friends. I was holding on for dear life...

THE BIRTH OF OUR FALSE SELF

Healthy human development is highly dependent upon having a genuine, loving bond with adults who are able to provide safety and support us in meeting our evolving needs. In the crucial early years of our life, if we have loving parents and a stable family, it helps to establish a solid foundation of healthy esteem and a growing, unique identity. At best, the connection with our Authentic Self remains fundamentally intact, and our life trajectory continues towards greater maturity and fulfillment.

All of us, however, go through some measure of traumatic circumstances, as the process of reckoning with life's challenges is an integral part of the hero's journey. If we do not receive adequate psychological and spiritual support at the time we are facing trauma—and few people do—we often develop wound patterns that culminate in the birth of our false self, also referred to as our adapted self. This is a psychological dynamic that takes place in virtually everyone's growth.

The false self is a fabricated identity created early in life for self-preservation in an attempt to protect ourselves from re-experiencing further trauma or stress in our close relationships. It is common for this false or "public" persona to portray an appearance of being OK in order to be socially acceptable. We learn to put on masks and adopt maladaptive behavioral patterns, allowing limiting aspects of ourselves to start leading our lives. As this occurs, we lose touch with our inner Light.

In our misguided attempts to shield ourselves from further pain, the false self deals with trauma by attempting to deny and repress our feelings. I experienced this acutely throughout my teens, and it had a devastating impact on my relationship with myself and others.

As my sister and brother spiraled out of control, I made a decisive shift away from what had been a steadily growing confidence in myself and my future into a constant state of anxiety. I was afraid that my life would go off the rails. My adapted persona, a mask of deception, took over and it held a limited, largely unconscious story about who I was. This darker picture, based on fear, created in me an increasing reticence to engage in life. It seemed that the world was no longer opening up to me, and I was no longer able to trust the process of life. I no longer felt safe.

My innate hopefulness was overridden by a new thought pattern that declared that life would always come up short, an entrenched fear that my life would continue falling apart. The young boy in me was no longer being seen, encouraged and supported by my parents, who had turned all their attention to the perpetual chaos and crises my siblings were creating. A growing sense of unworthiness festered inside of me. Internal doubt and self-judgment became rampant.

The false self is essentially guided by the judgmental mind with all its limitations, and the central dynamic that drives the false self is fear. Living from fear triggers the primal desire for safety and security above all else, which results in the maladapted patterns of self-protection I've been describing. The mind, when it wrestles control from our wise inner being, carries a fictitious authority. Fear holds us and our body spellbound, and its craving for outer acceptance motivates us to adopt a personality that we think will win us love and approval from others. Like the wavy mirrors we stand in front of at a carnival, fear is a lens that provides a distorted, false image of reality—and tragically corrodes our sense of connection with who we truly are.

All these life experiences, no matter how difficult, are also an essential part of our hero's journey. Ironically, a foundational key to becoming more anchored in our Authentic Self is learning to gently embrace and then step free from our false self's lead.

Invitation for Discovery

1. I invite you to reflect upon and identify one of the more significant traumas you faced in your childhood. Capture in your *Journal* the straightforward details as you remember them. Take some spacious time to describe your thoughts and feelings as you reflect upon these painful circumstances. As best as you can, bring the presence of your own loving compassion into a caring embrace of these thoughts and feelings.

2. Reflect upon and identify some of the core characteristics of your false self that may have developed as a result of facing these circumstances. See if you are able to recognize its underlying desire to protect and serve you as you were traversing this vulnerable passage in your life. It might also be healing to find some measure of gratitude for the process just the way it unfolded.

SAN QUENTIN

The metal gates slammed behind my parents and me as the guards ushered us through the prison to a small room. We passed through several security checkpoints. My body jumped every time a heavy steel door locked loudly behind us. I was 14 and we were making yet another visit to see Michael. This time he was at San Quentin, a maximum security prison located on the San Francisco Bay. We were told he was being held in solitary confinement because of a violent encounter with another inmate.

As we waited for Michael to appear, we sat facing a large plexiglass window, looking into an empty room with a single metal chair. Two large guards escorted him into the room. They sat him down in the chair, firmly handcuffed his wrists behind his back, then handcuffed his legs to the chair. The guards, who appeared anxious, then left Michael alone to visit with us.

His rage filled the room. With long, tangled hair and an unkempt beard, his skin covered in tattoos, he looked like Charles Manson to me. I was terrified of him. For what seemed like an eternity, we listened to him express his anger at the world through the microphone. We didn't know what to say. He looked like a trapped, wounded animal. Although his rage wasn't directed at us, my parents and I were once again in shock, and we sat there feeling helpless throughout the visit. After 20 minutes, the guards returned, removed Michael from the chair as he struggled against them, and took him away. As we drove home, my mother and father both wept. I sat in stunned silence, numb.

THE FALSE SELF REIGNS

Michael's journey is a powerful illustration of the birth of the false self. This adaptive self attempts to control the world to help us feel safe. All of us have faced circumstances in which we didn't feel safe. Trauma does not just happen to a few unlucky people, it happens to everyone—even under the best of circumstances.

Michael, who was severely beaten and emotionally abused as a young child by his biological father, grew to become a radical embodiment of the false self. He used the arrogance of his mind to convince himself that he belonged to a superior race—thus he thought he was justified in committing violence against African Americans. Fear and lack of control, seeded by the internalized violence of being on the receiving end of his father's brutality, fueled a life of cruelty.

When severe trauma takes place in early childhood, the long-term negative impact is often exponential. This was the case with my brother. The reality is that adults can much more readily change their circumstances under stressful conditions, but children cannot. They are basically at the mercy of adults' choices. Children also typically feel the painful impact of life's disturbances more deeply, as they have yet to develop adequate defense mechanisms to protect themselves.

My sister was also physically and emotionally abused early in her life by this same biological father. As the body's response to extraordinary trauma is often to crave comfort, it is common for survivors of severe abuse—if their deeper needs are not identified and met at the time—to eventually succumb to the powerful allure of mind-altering drugs and other addictive substances. This is an attempt to self-soothe and bring any measure of short-term relief to the flood of intense emotional pain they carry in their physical bodies.

Since the false self generally develops when we are very young, it has a tendency to carry infantile emotions and perspectives. The underlying anxiety and sense of alienation which flows from trauma often causes us to lose contact with our authentic nature. My sister had become trapped in the life of her false self. Filled with fear and shame, she was perpetually battling for survival and increasingly driven by the monstrous force of addiction.

While my family's circumstances were quite severe, most people on this planet are faced with the challenge of adapting to very real, painful experiences. We try to find the best way we can to survive, fit in and grow up. Along the way, most of us lose sight of who we really are.

THE WAKE OF THE STORM

For the next 15 years, my brother was in and out of prison and my sister's life was drowned in heroin addiction. My father, mother and I lived in constant fear that both of them might die at any time. We were emotionally devastated, and each of us went into survival mode in our own way. My parents simply didn't have the psychological understanding or finances to secure the therapeutic support we needed during this extended, tragic passage in our lives. And they had no internal resources left to support and encourage me in my development as a young man during such a critical stage in my life.

Everything that unfolded was particularly traumatizing for my mom. She was already carrying unhealed wounds from her own childhood. She was born to abusive, alcoholic parents, and ran away from home at age 14. Barely a teenager and completely on her own, she ended up pregnant and suffered through the trauma of having an abortion.

Pregnant again at age 15, she completed her pregnancy and then gave up the baby for adoption. In her late teens, my mom thought she'd found a healthy, safe relationship when she married a policeman. They had 2 children, Cathy and Michael. However, this man was quite disturbed himself and became physically and emotionally abusive to her and to both kids. He died suddenly in a motorcycle accident, which liberated my mom and siblings from his tyranny. A few years later, my mom opened to an experience of grace when she met my father and let him into her heart. They soon got married and I was born one year later. Despite the loving presence of my dad in her life, the devastation of my brother and sister's paths scarred her for the rest of her life.

Increasingly, my survival-based identity took on an unconscious pattern of attempting to be a hero to our family. My primary focus in life became trying to take care of my parents. I would do anything to make their lives easier. I tried to control myself and outer circumstances with my will as I didn't want my parents to experience any more pain. But my efforts to accomplish this meant pretending I was happy when I wasn't. The false self often has a tendency to portray itself as perfect, to not "make any mistakes," thus I became an excellent student with a perfect attendance record in school. In reality, of course, I was not invincible—underneath it all I was deeply wounded.

When we are not aligned with who we are, we can easily become addicted to comfort and a yearning for being accepted by others. The limited self, shaped by trauma, cannot effectively deal with the pressures, complications and demands of everyday life.

As the false self employs its reactive defenses, we can feel invisible and abandoned in our lives. This is often accompanied by a gnawing sense that we are flawed in some way. This false, unconscious story lives on until we find a genuine pathway towards healing and reconnection with our deeper nature.

LEARNING TO EMBRACE OUR FALSE SELF

Most people are unaware of the existence of their false self and the many ways it shows up in their lives. They mistakenly assume that who they are at their core is equivalent to their behavior and performance in the world. They become identified with their mask. Those who are conscious of their false self typically judge it harshly, and wage perpetual war against it. This is a trap, as it only serves to reinforce the powerful, dysfunctional influence of the false self.

I invite you to consider a different paradigm, one of becoming a conscious, compassionate student of your false self while simultaneously strengthening your connection with your Authentic Self. As you learn to do this, it is liberating for your false self to be embraced in its totality by your Authentic Self. This healing bond can assist you in becoming more integrated with your Authentic Self at your center.

"The false self doesn't want to give up being the center of our universe. It wants to engage us in a fight because that very act of taking a position, of opposing the false self, keeps the game going on its terms. But if, instead of fighting the false self, we love it without conditions, we enter the realm of the True Self. Automatically, the game ends."

~ John-Roger

As we're each here to learn different lessons in life, the wound patterning of the false self is distinctive for each person. As trauma binds energy, the protective nature of the false self often closes off the connection with our Authentic Self. The false self does not know how to truly lead, and most of us end up being held hostage by our minds. To become unbound and released from the energies of past trauma often requires a sustained process of healing, and I aspire that this book be a profound guide for you in that journey.

In deepening our understanding of the false self, it's critical to recognize that it has always had a distinct and noble purpose—to protect and serve us. The challenge isn't that we adapted to survive, but that we over-adapted to traumatic circumstances and remain trapped in our false identity long after it has served its purpose. Freeing ourselves from trauma and the reign of our false self is a central part of our Soul's curriculum.

The false self was never meant to be the driver of the car, but at some point in time it took over the steering wheel. Although it goes about its job faithfully, it secretly desires to be placed on a permanent leave of absence as we move on from the traumas of our past. As we progress on our healing journey, eventually the false self will admit to feeling overwhelmed by events and being incapable of rising to the task of genuine living. The false self will actually surrender its hold on us with the conscious arrival and loving leadership of our inner Light, the Authentic Self.

Invitation for Discovery

I invite you to close your eyes and take a few minutes to consider how your false self may present itself in your day-to-day life. Gently extend to it your empathy and understanding. Take the time to appreciate and honor your false self for its longstanding loyalty to you, for the ways it has genuinely endeavored to serve you in the best ways it has known. Capture in your Journal some of the specific ways your false self has served you in attempting to navigate traumatic circumstances.

WILD GEESE

by Mary Oliver

You do not have to be good.
You do not have to walk on your knees
for a hundred miles through the desert, repenting.
You only have to let the soft animal of your body
 love what it loves.

Tell me about despair, yours, and I will tell you mine.
Meanwhile the world goes on.
Meanwhile the sun and the clear pebbles of the rain
are moving across the landscapes,
over the prairies and the deep trees,
the mountains and the rivers.
Meanwhile the wild geese, high in the clean blue air,
are heading home again.

Whoever you are, no matter how lonely,
the world offers itself to your imagination,
calls to you like the wild geese, harsh and exciting —
over and over announcing your place
in the family of things.

CHAPTER 2

The Healing Begins: Turning Towards Our Authentic Self

"We often do not believe in ourselves until someone reveals that deep inside us something is valuable, worth listening to, worthy of our trust."

~ e.e. cummings

RESTORING TRUST IN RELATIONSHIP

The foundation of all life is relationship, for everything in the universe exists in relationship to everything else. The depth of fulfillment that we have in life is directly proportional to the level of genuine intimacy we have with ourselves, others and the world that surrounds us. Relationships flourish when they are built upon enduring trust.

By its nature, emotional trauma is the result of painful experiences in relationships. In essence, our trust becomes damaged and we lose faith in others. Here's the good news: the process of healing and releasing our trauma can be facilitated by consciously, steadily rebuilding healthy levels of trust—in our core relationship with ourselves and with others. No matter how dark or longstanding our early life experiences, the healing presence and guiding wisdom of the Authentic Self can be accessed to assist us in the restoration of this trust at any point in our lives.

Thankfully, a steady flow of healing life experiences found their way to my doorstep in the midst of the painful chaos going on in my family. These glimmers of Light were most welcome and served to guide me on my path.

JOHNNY WILKES

When I was 13 years old, I was trying to fix a broken carburetor on my off-road motorcycle and was feeling frustrated that I couldn't do it. By this time in my early teens, my pattern of sudden explosive outbursts was already well ingrained. Each and every time they occurred, seemingly out of nowhere, nobody wanted to come near me. Johnny Wilkes, my dad's close friend, was an exception to the rule. He saw me beginning to lose my temper over the carburetor and calmly approached me. He leaned down next to me and said, "I can help you with that." His voice was gentle and compassionate.

As we worked side-by-side, he continued,"I understand why you're frustrated. I can get frustrated like that, too. I trust that you and I can work together to fix this." As he spoke, my entire body relaxed. He was patient with me. I felt his kindness and support as we worked side-by-side and fixed the carburetor. It was the first time I had ever experienced anyone supporting me this way while I was in the midst of a meltdown.

KINDNESS HEALS

Johnny's patience, kindness and love reached in, past my pain and shame, and touched my heart. It was deeply healing to have someone graciously and sincerely enter into my world just as I was about to escalate into an angry explosion. Johnny responded to my distress with a simple act of acceptance and support. This single encounter pierced through a thick layer of shame I'd been carrying since my pattern of temper tantrums had begun. After this experience, I gradually learned how to access my own calm whenever I would get emotionally upset. The presence of Johnny's healing compassion in that moment made an indelible impression upon my life.

The truth is that trauma doesn't have to define you. If approached with compassion and effective healing techniques, it can lead you back home to your Authentic Self. You are not forever bound to your trauma. You can get past the past. Genuine, life-giving trust can be restored inside yourself and in your relationships with others.

Invitation for Discovery

I invite you to take some time to reflect upon the arc of your life and identify a precious memory of when someone extended their caring to you in a way that you found moving and healing. Perhaps their compassion or generosity showed up when you most needed it. Capture your reflections of this meaningful memory in your *Journal.* You might consider reaching out to this person and expressing your thanks to them. Even if they are no longer alive, they are alive within you, and you may find that the process of expressing your heart to them in words to be profoundly healing.

HERE COMES THE SUN

It was early morning on Christmas Day. It was 1969, and I was 14 years old. My parents took me to the Greyhound station and put me on a bus to visit my grandparents in Bakersfield. It was a 3-hour trip north and I'd never taken a long trip by myself before. I boarded the bus wondering if I would be safe. I didn't talk to anyone. My mind was racing, and although I wasn't sure if taking this trip was a good idea, I was also excited.

After I got settled in my window seat and the bus started rolling, I remembered my final Christmas gifts in my backpack. I had saved them to open during the trip. I eagerly unwrapped them and discovered that my parents had given me a Radio Shack cassette player, a set of headphones, and a cassette of the Beatles "Abbey Road" album, which had just been released. I'll never forget the experience of listening to that album for the very first time. One song in particular touched me to the core, "Here Comes the Sun," which I listened to over and over again.

As we headed north through the mountains, away from my family and all its chaos, it felt like I was actually beginning to breathe my own air. My anxiety and the rattling of my thoughts slowly faded. Peace settled over me as I looked out the bus window and listened to that song for what seemed like an eternity. Somehow, on this trip, I found myself feeling more confident and hopeful than I had in a long time. I relaxed and started taking fuller breaths. It felt like I was being rewarded by my parents, by life itself. My world expanded in a small but very real way on this journey. I was finally emerging from the darkness into the Light.

This trip marked my glorious awakening to the healing power of music. I started collecting 331/3 RPM records. The profound passions of our Authentic Self reside within us whether we acknowledge them or not. Often they get buried under learned behaviors and the self-protective strategies of the false self. However, if we allow it, each new experience of abiding trust can reconnect us more fully with ourself.

By focusing on the things that soothe your Soul and aid your healing, the negative conclusions of the false self—along with any binding shame you are carrying—can steadily dissolve over time. With each experience of healing, you anchor new levels of safety and resilience. Steadily, over time, your deeper nature becomes the solid ground you stand on.

Invitation for Discovery

I invite you to record in your *Journal* the details of a truly memorable road trip or experience of travel in your life. What about it was so meaningful? Were you going through an important or challenging passage? Did music or a specific song play into this memory? What song? When was the last time you listened to this song? What emotions does this song evoke in you today?

INITIATION IN THE DESERT

I was 17. My dad and I often loaded our dirt bikes in the back of his truck and headed out to the Mojave Desert. Riding motorcycles on weekends was one of our ways of coping. The desert was open and spacious and had such a gentle and peaceful presence. It was so quiet and beautiful out there.

My father, who had Type 1 diabetes, had to eat his meals at regular intervals during each day or face the threat of diabetic shock or death. So we never went out on a ride on our dirt bikes without packing adequate food for him.

One late afternoon, we were out riding in the desert longer than expected and he had mistakenly left his food back at the truck. As the sun went down, as happens in the desert, it quickly turned quite dark and cold. At a certain point, we could only see a few feet in front of us, and then we realized that we were lost. For safety's sake, we laid our bikes on the desert floor and walked. We had no idea where the truck was.

My father, uncharacteristically, was suddenly overcome by panic. "I have no idea where we are, it's getting very cold, and I don't have my food," he moaned tearfully.

As I felt him trembling, something inside of me rose up in response to this life-or-death challenge. Surprisingly, I found myself feeling immensely confident and relaxed, and I said, "Dad, I know where the truck is, just follow me."

I had no idea where this strong knowing came from, but I trusted it. My dad felt the sincerity of my reassurance and calmed down. Following my intuitive guidance for direction, we walked in the pitch dark for about 30 minutes and arrived safely back at the truck. My dad immediately gulped down the food he needed, and later we went back to pick up our motorcycles, using the truck's headlights to guide us.

This powerful experience in the desert was an initiation into adulthood for me. It was a sudden arrival of my connection with the power of intuition, the wise knowing of my Authentic Self.

With this experience, my relationship with my father fundamentally shifted. I was deeply honored by this unexpected opportunity to demonstrate my inner strength and fulfill my desire to be the son he could really count on during a time of real challenge. From that point on, I took the lead in our relationship. Up until that time, whenever we rode in the desert, my dad would ride behind me, protecting me. After this experience, I became the protector and always rode behind him. We both knew something had changed, but we didn't talk about it. My father saw and trusted me in a new way.

Beginning to connect with the reality of your wise knowing, in undeniable and profound ways, is a blessing beyond measure. As you steadily reconnect with the core qualities of the Authentic Self, the false self relaxes and releases its fearful grip. You re-open your heart to the glorious sensation of trusting yourself, with greater confidence to navigate your life.

Invitation for Discovery

I invite you to identify a painful time in your life when you were facing challenging circumstances, and then something unexpectedly positive occurred. Maybe your intuitive voice revealed itself to you in a surprising way, or someone had faith in you when things looked darkest. Capture in your *Journal* your experience of this memory as it unfolded, as well as any impact it may have had upon your life.

MY FATHER'S ILLNESS

I was 18. My dad had just been diagnosed with cancer. I remember exactly where I was in the kitchen when he came home from his doctor's appointment. The doctor had told my father that he had a growth inside his abdomen the size of a small basketball and he needed surgery immediately. When my dad relayed this shocking news to me and my mom, his face was ashen. I can still remember the bitter taste that filled my mouth the moment he told us.

After the surgery, a biopsy confirmed that a malignant cancer had spread throughout his body. The doctors said he had approximately 6 months to live. They said that there was no treatment available to cure him, and suggested he begin making arrangements for hospice care. We were all numb. After all we had traversed with my brother and sister, now we were being asked to face this.

Given how close I was to my dad, I immediately quit my job and college because I wanted to spend the last months of my father's life by his side. Amazingly, he responded to his bleak prognosis with an inspiring, wholehearted and determined will to live. He signed up for an experimental chemotherapy treatment from Japan that he hoped would give him more time. Despite horrific side effects, he never complained and called each day a "freebie." Although we were already so close to each other, my dad and I continued to get closer.

It may have been the rigorous treatments, or his indestructible will to live, but to everyone's surprise, especially his doctor, his condition dramatically improved.

Building on this stupendous news, one day my father decided that he wanted to attend junior college classes with me. What an extraordinary opportunity this provided both of us. I can still remember standing in the registration line and looking up at the list of classes we wanted to take together. Our drives to school in the early morning were precious, because we both knew that these might be our final months together. Each afternoon we would eat our lunch together at the college dining hall, and I remember many of our teachers and newfound friends letting us know that they only wished they could go to school with their father. My Dad and I would do our homework and study for upcoming exams together at night. It was a poignant passage in our relationship. Although we were father and son, it always seemed to me like we were close brothers. As neither of us knew how long he would be alive, this unforgettable time of walking side-by-side in our lives meant everything to us.

HARVESTING GOLD

My dad exemplified someone who accepted and embraced change. He brought a wholeheartedness and radiant gratitude to life's most challenging circumstances. Despite facing a death sentence from his doctors, he seemed to come more alive in his Authentic Self from the moment his cancer diagnosis arrived. Miraculously, he reached and passed the 2-year mark following his diagnosis and was only getting healthier. His enthusiastic immersion in the moment and appreciation for the gift of life was contagious. Given that my dad and I were together almost 24/7 during this period, his pure gratitude for living steadily dissolved the levels of distrust and anxiety I was carrying. We were both getting a hold of our resilience. Thankfully, as I traversed junior college, the limiting unconscious patterns of my false self continued loosening their grip on me.

Sometimes life's passages can be incredibly dark and painful, but if the learnings from them are harvested in a genuine and honorable way, we can grow in leaps and bounds through difficult times. As it turned out, my dad's cancer became a blessing in our family. Despite my brother and sister's on-going challenges, a healing and trusting relationship kept deepening between me and both of my parents. As South Africa's Nelson Mandela demonstrated in the face of decades of adversity and imprisonment, the Authentic Self knows triumph and can choose not to be defeated by this world.

MY FIRST LOVE

Even though I had a warm relationship with my dad when I first entered junior college, I still didn't have any close friends and was mostly closed off to everyone else. I was just trying to move on with my life despite the constant drama of my brother and sister, which continued to haunt me and my parents.

I was 19 when I met a woman named Zena in my second year of classes. She was tall, beautiful and one of the sweetest people I had ever met. I was swept away, and one day finally had the courage to ask her out on a date. In that moment when she said yes, my life dramatically changed course. We read poetry together at the end of that first date, and I experienced an extraordinary opening of my heart. I wasn't aware of how emotionally closed off I had become. We continued dating and I was shocked by how quickly she came to love me so much.

Zena was a lifeline that had arrived in my life right when I needed it most. One of the most extraordinary moments of my life took place when we made love for the first time. This intimate experience awakened in me a profound presence of tenderness, strength and expansion that seemed like it was from another dimension.

It was so delicious to be falling rapturously in love. I remember Zena and me taking an unforgettable week-long road trip up the California Big Sur coastline in my Dodge van. The entire time, it was as if the heavens had opened up and currents of joy were coursing through us. The rich flow of memories from this trip, including spending treasured time together in magical San Francisco, will always be emblazoned in my heart.

She and I shared many interests including a love of nature, poetry and a mutual calling to become licensed psychotherapists. We were together for almost 6 years, and during this time we both completed the same bachelor's and master's degree programs in counseling psychology.

HEALING TRAUMA

Having a brave willingness to risk reaching out to create new, healthy relationships is essential for the healing of trauma. Zena played a crucial role in my life by setting into motion my process of recovery from my many years of family trauma. In this new encounter, I gradually let go of my protective behaviors and opened to greater levels of trust—and to the presence of my Authentic Self. To experience being seen and loved for who I was began to transform my relationship with myself and the world. Genuine intimacy is profoundly healing and restores our belief that our birthright is to live a deeply fulfilling life.

"In everyone's life, at some time, our inner fire goes out. It is then burst into flame by an encounter with another human being. We should all be thankful for those people who rekindle the inner spirit."

~ Albert Schweitzer

MY AUTHENTIC SELF AWAKENS

I had no idea what I wanted to do with my life when I arrived for that first day of classes in my second year of junior college. I was sitting in a psychology class when the teacher walked in and began to welcome us. At that very moment, an older man stuck his head through the doorway and said, "Fuck you, Mike. Fuck you." His comment was addressed to the teacher. We were all shocked.

Mike said back to him, "No, fuck you," and a verbal fight erupted between them.

We were all stunned. All the students were like, "Whoa." Then our teacher and this man actually started wrestling on the floor in front of the class, growling and yelling at each other.

Finally, Mike actually picked up the other man and threw him out of the classroom, yelling, "Get the fuck out of here."

He then turned to us and said, "Now, everybody write down what you just saw." He didn't tell us why he was asking us to do this, but gave us 10 minutes to write and then said, "Okay. Let's hear from a number of you."

As different students shared what they had observed, it truly surprised us that there were many different versions of the same event. He then said, "Now, let's talk about the subjective nature of reality. My name is Mike Gardner. I'll be your teacher." At that moment, we all realized he had staged the fight as the opening of our first lesson.

Mike was a rare and inspiring teacher who deeply activated my depth and intelligence. For a few years, I'd been drawn to take a psychology class, as I'd hoped it might provide me with insight into my intense emotional pain. Throughout his class, because of his radical aliveness and insight, my calling towards the arenas of psychology and personal growth steadily grew. Looking back, it is clear that the dark period of my teens had catapulted me towards discovering my life's work. The course of my life journey made an astonishing turn as a result of Mike Gardner's generous leadership.

Invitation for Discovery

I invite you to identify a teacher who inspired you and perhaps changed the course of your life. What was this teacher's name? What memories do you associate with this teacher's presence in your life? Describe in your *Journal* the specific qualities this teacher embodied that had a powerful impact upon you. Consider reaching out to them to express your heartfelt thanks for the contribution they made to your life.

PRESENCE

by Paul Williams

You have a power
that has nothing
to do with what you do
or what you say
or who you know or what you know
or where you are or what you
look like or your skills
or your talents
or what you have.
It is the power of your presence.
It is the heat and light from your burning log.
And it touches everyone who
comes in contact with you....

CHAPTER 3

Nine Signature Qualities of Our Authentic Self

"Know your fire, your light, and offer it creatively to others who are walking with you."

~ Brugh Joy M.D.

The purpose of this chapter is to familiarize you with what I consider to be the nine universal qualities of the Authentic Self. As you embrace these core qualities to an ever-greater degree, as well as other qualities that stir you, the full spectrum of your deeper nature reveals itself. Your connection with these intertwined qualities evolves and expands over time, for embodying your Authentic Self is a lifelong unfoldment.

1) FINDING TREASURE IN EVERY PERSON & SITUATION

When I was 9 years old, our neighborhood trash pickup day was Monday. People put their trash bins out the night before. So at the crack of dawn on Monday mornings, before the trash trucks came, I'd go around the neighborhood pulling my red wagon behind me. I became quite adept at quietly and briskly going through people's trash bins in semi-darkness, and to my delight often found some of the most wonderful things they had thrown away. What I reveled in most was the moment when I would catch a glimpse of an object that to most people was viewed as worthless, but that I recognized to be a hidden treasure.

Whether it was an old bicycle, clock, chair, etc., I would call the things I picked out "keepers" and would excitedly take them home. The next stage in my process was spending time after school each day fixing up all the things I had collected. Take an old bicycle, for example: I can remember taking the whole thing apart, sanding the frame, hanging it from the railing of the garage door and spray painting it a gorgeous metallic purple. With my dad's help, I cleaned all of the bearings in solvent and lathered them in thick new grease before re-installing them along with new foot pedals. I often put on different colored grips on the handle bars and cool new tires if needed. At this point, the bicycle was transformed into something uniquely beautiful. And so it was that I had a weekly ritual of carefully reconditioning all my newfound "keepers."

The following weekend I would go around the block riding the renovated bicycle, with the other resurrected items carefully laid out in my red wagon towed behind me, offering them for sale to my neighbors. I was known as the kid in the neighborhood with the "wagon store." Quite often, as someone would be looking over my wares, they would see something I was selling that struck them as very familiar. They'd say to me, "I used to have a bike just like that." (Of course, it often was their old bike, and they were buying it back from me at a premium!) I would simply smile to myself...and wouldn't say a word. I rejoiced in this weekly ritual of finding treasures and earning money by doing something I loved.

I have come to understand that it was my Authentic Self who would look at a rusty bicycle and, in my imagination, see it glistening with everything I would do to make it beautiful again. This capacity to see the hidden potential is reflected in the sculpting technique of the Renaissance artist, Michelangelo. He described how he could see an exquisite human figure trapped in a block of marble, and then remove layer after layer of stone to uncover the figure encased within. This technique spoke to the fact that he was perceiving the world differently than most people.

In a similar way, in my early 20's I had the realization that those adults I encountered in my life whose eyes were not shining were indeed carrying a powerful Light within them—it had just been buried and forgotten under a lot of pain. Like Michelangelo, you can cultivate the capacity to see the Light of the Authentic Self within everyone you meet, even if they are blind to this presence themselves.

When someone comes to you in distress, you can bring your primary focus to seeing and connecting with their loving essence that, with practice, becomes readily evident beyond the current difficulties playing out in their lives. This way of perceiving is particularly valuable in the common occurrence when a cloak of tragedy in someone's life is veiling their genuine treasure. Every person's True Self has the transformative capability of recognizing treasure in all the ways it surrounds us.

It is a profoundly rewarding experience to silently hold space for another's beauty. Connecting with the treasure within every person you encounter and, at best, helping them to touch into their own treasure, is a source of pure wealth and joy.

Invitation for Discovery

a) I invite you to identify one of the more difficult passages in your life journey. As you reflect upon this time in your life, see if you can look at it through fresh eyes such that you recognize the treasure or gift that was made available to you as a result of this challenging situation.

b) Take some time to reflect upon someone you've known (or perhaps even yourself) who, while facing serious and even tragic adversity, continued to be in touch with their shining inner Light and even grew stronger through it all. Honor them in your *Journal* by capturing the ways that they harvested treasures even while enduring painful experiences.

2) IMMERSION IN THE MOMENT

Although you may have forgotten it, you were immersed in your Authentic Self during the first few years of your life. You came into this world drenched in it, not knowing there was any other way to be. A young child is 100% authentic and couldn't be inauthentic if they tried.

This season of immersion in infants has often been described as a sensation of eternity, a feeling of unboundedness. Every child starts out in this state of oceanic consciousness, a sea of sensation and emotion with no boundaries at all. They cannot distinguish themselves from their mother or any other outside object.

Over time, we each develop an ego, which is essentially a boundary marker, a delineator of ourselves as distinct from every other thing. As we mature, most of us lose the ability to contact the earlier oceanic feeling because of a sense of separateness created from identifying with this limited ego.

The flow of the Authentic Self is a here-and-now process. As you learn to let go of past concerns and stop generating fear and anxiety about the future, you are more available to the dynamic, moment-by-moment flow of creation in the present. When you experience these vibrant and relaxing energies, you can learn to direct the wisdom they carry into every area of your life. This enables you to make more aligned choices, resulting in a more fulfilling future.

Invitation for Discovery

The next time you find yourself in the presence of an infant or toddler, I invite you to consider spending 10-15 minutes observing and taking in the rich quality of their immersion as they interact with their world. Capture your observations in your *Journal*.

3) WISE KNOWING

The Authentic Self has woven within it a consciousness of natural knowing that resides far beyond the realm of the mind. It is an intuitive intelligence, and its guidance often comes as a flow of inspiration or creativity—and is much more available to us when the chatter of the mind has subsided. Having a strong relationship with this natural knowing leads to making wise choices.

Each of us has unique ways of attuning to our intuitive voice that resonate with the presence of truth. You may remember carefully turning the knob on an FM radio to the left or right until you landed in that center sweet spot on the dial where the music sounds crystal clear with no static. Our relationship with our intuition is much like this. As you learn to listen to and act upon your wisdom, with patience and fine tuning, your connection to it will strengthen.

One key to deepening our relationship with wise knowing is to embrace the experience of *not knowing*. In our culture, when we are feeling insecure, it is commonplace for people to get caught in an unconscious pattern of thinking, or pretending, that we have all the answers. Those with this approach to life often have an investment in how they appear to others and are hesitant to admit when they don't know something. It can be a huge relief to let go of this pattern as we discover the power and freedom of acknowledging, "I don't know." Ironically, when we embrace *not knowing*, our *natural knowing* often becomes more accessible. The wisdom cultivated in this practice is empowering and becomes more available as you begin taking action on the inner guidance you receive.

Invitation for Discovery

I invite you to take a few relaxing breaths. Consider the possibility that there is a wisdom inside of you that is far greater than your intellect. This is your ever-present and available wise knowing. Now, identify a life challenge you are currently facing. As you reflect upon this challenge, attune inwardly—in whatever way that seems most natural to you—and open to receive whatever guidance may be flowing to you from this center of knowing. How does your wisdom suggest you respond to this situation? Is there any new perspective of the situation being gifted to you by this guidance?

Write in your *Journal* whatever your wise knowing communicates with you. Know that this intuitive aspect of your Authentic Self is available as often as you call upon it. There is no "right" way to experience this inner guidance. It may come as an actual voice, as an image or idea, as a sensation, or as any combination of these. The intuitive process varies from person to person, and from situation to situation within our own consciousness.

4) LOVING COMPASSION

Compassion is the primary universal quality of the Authentic Self, and is considered among the greatest of virtues in all the major spiritual and religious traditions. The healing power of compassion is best exemplified by those who can meet someone who has committed a heinous crime and respond with genuine empathy and a healing presence. We have all read those stories of extraordinary people who meet the murderer of their loved one and bring forward only genuine love and forgiveness. Experiencing trauma often results in a painfully closed heart, with little capacity to recognize and respond to another's humanity. Yet, in the balm of deep compassion, both self-judgment and shaming of others are transformed into love.

We are all, individually and collectively, on a healing journey. The most powerful territory for transformational healing is in your relationship with yourself. You arrived in this world without a map and throughout your life you have faced many challenges. You are naturally capable of attuning to the comfort of your heart, and continually have opportunities to bring your tender compassion towards any trauma, judgment or pain you may be carrying. For many, the process of opening to your own softness is perhaps the hardest yet the most crucial learning in this lifetime. Truly, you are capable of blessing yourself by bringing love to those places inside that are crying out for it.

Tethering ourselves to the Authentic Self allows for an intimate relationship with our core of love. We can carry a quality of healing empathy and act in kind and affirming ways toward ourselves and others. Kindness, then, is compassion put into action.

Kindness is offering encouragement or helping someone up when they have fallen—and offering a way for them to stand taller and in greater peace. Awakening to our compassion, we find a gateway to the fuller expression of our love. Indeed, we all carry a rich reservoir of loving compassion within. As we choose to affirm and exercise it, it grows more abundant and free flowing.

Invitation for Discovery

I invite you to take a moment to identify a specific quality or behavior of yours that you currently find unacceptable. Then, take a moment to tune into the energies of your own tender compassion. You can do this by sensing your heart or by simply recalling how you feel in the presence of someone you dearly love. This could be a child or it could be an animal companion. Breathing deeply, let that feeling of caring grow in you. Now extend this healing presence to that quality or behavior you have judged and are learning to embrace. See yourself warmly accepting this inner aspect just as it is, without condemnation. Your underlying communication to this quality or behavior is one of reassurance, letting it know that it is safe. Notice how this formerly unacceptable condition may soften in response to your healing compassion. For limiting patterns that are very entrenched, the process of accessing our own healing presence may need to be exercised gently and steadily over time. Capture your experience in your *Journal*.

"What wound did ever heal but by degrees?"
~ Shakespeare, *Othello*

5) THE ETERNAL STUDENT

One morning my kindergarten teacher rolled a chick incubator into our classroom. It was a large glass dome mounted on a table. Inside the dome were 9 white chicken eggs with a heat lamp over them. The teacher told us that baby chicks would hatch out of the eggs in about 3 weeks. Those eggs became the center of our young lives. We were so curious about how something could be living inside of them. How could they breath? We were riveted as the teacher answered all of our questions.

One morning, as we all crowded around the warm incubator, teetering on our toes to get a good peek, we saw cracks appearing on the outside of the eggs. Our teacher told us this was called pipping. Lo and behold, by the time we got to school the next day, we squealed with delight at the sight of the chicks at different stages of hatching out of their shells. Some had just emerged and were wet and exhausted, while others were fluffy and chirpy, and a few were walking for the first time.

One of the most extraordinary qualities of the Authentic Self is that it is imminently curious. Its purpose in life is to gain experience. In a child-like way, it leads with innocence and is always looking at life through fresh eyes with an insatiable desire to participate and discover. On this planet, we are primarily here as students. Earth is a school where we are here to learn and grow.

Invitation for Discovery

The power of curiosity applies to all walks of life. Let's take an opportunity to shine the Light of the eternal student on your relationships. I invite you to identify a disagreement you had or are having with someone important in your life. As you reflect upon the specific nature of this disagreement, consider whether you might have been coming from a desire to be right or a perceived need to defend your position. If so, you might remind yourself about the power of being a student who is genuinely open to learning something new. You might also reflect upon the following question, "What is this relationship teaching me about myself?" Explore whether your curiosity sparks a shift in your inner attitude and how you might relate to the other person. Write your reflections in your *Journal*.

6) VULNERABILITY

To be vulnerable means to allow yourself to fully experience the vibrant presence of Life as it reveals itself moment to moment. We have a tendency to think of vulnerability as a weakness, something to be avoided. In actuality, vulnerability is at the core of authenticity, and is a strength that endows you with power. Rooted in safety and openness, it is an exquisite faculty of perception you've been given that serves as a doorway to greater intimacy in your inner and outer life. You can learn to cultivate transparency and allow it to inform the way you operate in the world.

"Vulnerability is the underlying, ever-present and abiding undercurrent of our natural state."

~ David Whyte

Each day you are given the opportunity to embrace whatever you're experiencing in life and to find strength in your vulnerability. This is an easy affair when you are experiencing something pleasurable. However, your interior world, like the natural world, has its own seasons and "weather patterns," including periods of contraction, darkness and pain. When you give such deep feelings permission to be experienced, they can powerfully transform and uplift you. Cultivating the strength of heart to honor the vulnerability of human life, amidst all its ups and downs, fuels aliveness.

A central key in this process is openness. In particular, we can open to the tender energies of our heart that are more accepting, healing and forgiving. Being human, we routinely stray from these heartfelt energies, and when we do, it's like being locked outside our home late at night. We peer in the windows and see logs burning in the fireplace—yet because we've misplaced our keys we're stranded in the cold and dark.

It's important to recognize that living a more robust vulnerability also calls for surrendering to your joy and expansive sense of well-being. It's a radical act to allow genuine happiness to flow through you. Initially it can be frightening to allow yourself to experience new levels of sheer pleasure, as it can feel like you are out of control.

"Vulnerability is having the courage to show up and be seen when we have no control over the outcome. What makes you vulnerable makes you beautiful."

~ Brene Brown

Embracing vulnerability also requires that you cultivate a relationship with silence and spaciousness, which involves dropping down into your body and the presence of your stillness. There you can access deeper levels of your truth. The key is to get more comfortable with not feeling comfortable.

One of history's great leaders, Abraham Lincoln, is known to have given himself tremendous permission to experience his own vulnerability and suffering throughout his life—while simultaneously opening himself to Divine assistance. His intimate relationship with his own melancholy deepened his connection with his humanity and wisdom, and contributed to his extraordinary stewardship of our country through its darkest hours.

Invitation for Discovery

a) How might you describe your current relationship with your vulnerability? Consider times when you are dealing with an area of weakness and fallibility in yourself and have failed to meet your own goals and standards. Do you tend towards being a harsh critic or a compassionate partner offering forgiveness to yourself with a gentle invitation to do better next time?

b) I invite you to take the time to identify specific ways you might be willing to embrace new expressions of vulnerability and softness in your relationship with yourself and others. Capture your responses in your *Journal*.

7) EMBRACING ONENESS

The core limiting pattern all human beings deal with is the illusion of separation—a painful sense of disconnection from oneself, from others, and from the Spirit of Life itself. This false paradigm of separateness, in which an unconscious conclusion is made that we are somehow fundamentally unworthy as a human being, feeds a wide range of human suffering.

The capacity to embrace unity, within ourselves and the world around us, is the quality of the Authentic Self that empowers us to awaken from this illusion. It flows from a very different paradigm, one which recognizes that we are equipped with an internal and eternal Light that is our deepest nature and is ever-available to guide us.

What feeds the illusion of separateness is the pervasive cultural conditioning that we exist only inside our own skin. Quantum physicists have proven otherwise. They have discovered that there is no way of separating a human organism from its external environment—that all of life is interconnected. Our very skin is actually a dynamic and inter-relational gateway in which energies traverse between our inner world and the outer world. The contagion of a virus that begins in one part of the world and then quickly travels around the globe, affecting the health and well-being of billions, is a perfect illustration of our interconnectedness in a very physical way.

True wealth does not mean having lots of things, it means being in intimate communication with the essence of all things. In the immortal words of Alan Watts, "We are each continuous with the Universe as a wave is continuous with the ocean." When we experience with this felt sense of this unity, we feel a gratefulness that lifts us beyond all division.

"There is an invisible workmanship that reconciles discordant elements and makes them move in one society."

~ William Wordsworth

Invitation for Discovery

I invite you to take a few minutes to reflect upon a profound experience in your life, a time in which you found yourself unmistakably moved, where something deep in you came alive. Perhaps you remember being present for the birth of a child, or having an epiphany during a retreat or workshop, or were immersed in an intimate relationship where nothing in the world mattered outside of what was happening between the two of you, or you entered into an expansive state of timelessness in nature. Capture in your *Journal* the specific ways you experienced being connected in oneness with a Presence larger than yourself, and how it may have affected your outlook on life and subsequent choices.

8) GENEROUS LEADERSHIP

Teachers, artists and entrepreneurs who are masterful in their particular field have been honing their craft for years. With a profound love for what they do, they've been absorbed in the process of refining their gift of expression. This evolution into mastery is driven by the fulfillment that comes from expressing their Authentic Self with ever-greater levels of clarity and creativity.

Have you ever had a teacher who dynamically engaged you in their classroom? Their identity was not driven by ego but by their passion for creating a fertile learning environment. They were not there to tell you everything they knew, but to be an active partner and guide on your own journey of discovery. The goal of such teachers is to fuel the fires of curiosity within their students so that their passion for learning will burn undiminished throughout their lifetime. Teachers like this are rare. Mike Gardner, my college psychology teacher, was one such teacher. They make a powerful, lasting contribution to the quality of their students' lives, and they themselves never tire of learning.

Like great teachers, inspirational leaders are simultaneously dedicated students. The East Indian leader, Mahatma Gandhi, was well known for not expecting his followers to do anything he wasn't willing to do himself. He was once approached by a mother who asked him how her daughter could heal a physical illness she was facing. After carefully considering her question, he asked her to come back to see him in 2 weeks for his answer. When she returned 2 weeks later, he told her that her daughter needed to stop eating sugar. The mother, somewhat exasperated, asked him, "Why didn't you tell me that 2 weeks ago?" Gandhi replied, "2 weeks ago I was eating sugar."

Evolved leaders inspire by example. They carry an unmistakable shining Light and inner strength of character, and act with compassion and knowing. We are instinctively called to follow them and to learn from them. Even as they continue to grow into greater mastery, they serve as catalysts.

As you become more anchored in your Soul, your Authentic Self, you naturally begin stepping into generous leadership in service to yourself and to those around you. Like a small acorn that grows into a huge oak tree, leadership is an instinctive potential you carry in your bones. It is your destiny as a wise creator.

"One thing I know: the only ones among you who will be really happy are those who have sought and found how to serve."

~ Albert Schweitzer

Mature leadership involves prioritizing the welfare of all those impacted by your actions and becoming a steward to something larger than yourself. Your life becomes increasingly led by intelligent and sensitive choices, and you harvest challenges as fuel for growth. Difficulties in relationships of all kinds become recognized as opportunities to strengthen and expand your bonds of care. Living into true leadership, you can evolve by viewing your relationships as mirrors—and look to see how you might be exhibiting the very behaviors that you object to in others. With generous leadership, it is no longer a matter of *whether* you will you choose to serve, it's about *who* and *how* you are guided to serve.

Invitation for Discovery

a) I invite you to identify someone who has inspired you and positively impacted your life through their generous leadership. As you reflect upon this person, pay attention to your inner experience. Consider how this person has inspired your own impulse to be a compassionate leader. Note in your *Journal* some of the specific thoughts and feelings that stir inside as you re-visit how this person touched your life.

b) In what ways have you recently been a generous leader in your life? It is important to note that leadership may manifest in big ways and small ways. Some examples include serving your home by caring for the yard, supporting your co-workers or clients, enjoying your children just as they are, tending to your physical body, receiving love and support from your family, taking time to be present with hurt feelings inside yourself, or honoring your call to send someone a handwritten card of appreciation. Generous leadership is more about the loving Spirit we bring to our service than about who or what we serve.

9) GRATITUDE

After our lives were intertwined for 6 fulfilling years, and just after Zena and I received our masters' degrees, my life took a radical turn towards spirituality. As this core dimension wasn't part of Zena's path at the time, we mutually chose to part ways even though we loved each other immensely. The grief of our loss ran deep, and the memory of the final time we made love to each other will be with me forever.

Zena played such a crucial role in assisting me as I began recovering from my years of family trauma. During our rich companionship, which included supporting each other in completing our studies, I was initiated into a compassionate and generous world beyond mere survival. Throughout my life, I have carried a depth of gratitude for her immense contribution to my life journey. At a time on my path when I needed it most, she was my saving grace…

A consciousness of gratitude is more than just focusing on the positive. It is a recognition of a deeper reality that life is always unfolding in ways that bring us blessings and the opportunity to learn. Sincere thankfulness is a potent energy field and a foundational vehicle for transforming our lives. Whenever we consciously choose to enter its gravitational presence, it automatically begins to dissolve the anxieties of our mind. It has an uncanny way of ushering us into the present moment, into the healing energies of our heart.

Gratitude and grace are intimately connected, and welcoming their presence into our lives requires that we remain open and vulnerable. Activating a consciousness of gratitude brings us back to the recognition that life is a precious gift continuously waiting to be revealed and seen anew. It magically reunites us with the presence of the Authentic Self.

Practices of people coming together to give thanks are found the world over. These rituals are intended to activate the blessings of gratitude both in spite of and because of the troubles of the world. Feeling and expressing gratitude affirms our recognition that there is an underlying wholeness and enduring sanctity to life.

Thousands of scientific studies have demonstrated a significant increase in relaxation and equanimity among people who regularly express genuine gratitude. Just by embodying thankfulness, we became healthier and more peaceful. The world opens up to us when we live in a space of gratitude. When we practice appreciation, our perception of the world seems to glow a bit brighter—with a snowball effect that lights up the world around us.

There is always something to be grateful for, even when life gets hard. When times are tough, whether we are having a bad day or stuck in what may feel like an endless rut, it can be difficult to access a consciousness of gratitude. Yet, these times are when doing so can be most impactful.

There are blessings to be found everywhere. As you choose to bring your focus to being grateful, you notice that every breath is a miracle. The state of genuine gratitude is one of innocence and receptivity. In a self-fulfilling phenomenon, the more you open yourself to appreciate life, the more you make yourself accessible to the steady flow of generosity that resides all around you.

Gratitude is a powerful medicine. It is a choice, an attitude, an approach to life. Gratitude for your journey just as it is unfolding is not determined by what is actually taking place in any given moment; rather it is that you practice gratitude in the moment regardless of what is going on. Celebrating your next breath is not simply about taking in oxygen. It's about the astonishing fact that you are breathing at all, that you recognize it comes from a mysterious higher source, and that miraculously you are alive.

"If there is gratitude in your heart, then there will be tremendous sweetness in your eyes."

~ Sri Chinmoy

Invitation for Discovery

a) I invite you to take a few minutes to capture in writing 4 or 5 things that you are sincerely grateful for about yourself and your life—just the way it is.

b) I invite you to identify some of the ways that you might experience and express gratitude in your life on a more consistent basis. One possibility, among many, is to begin keeping a *Gratitude Journal* in which you capture expressions of heartfelt thanks in the evening when you get into bed. Reflecting with sincere appreciation upon the flow of experiences from your day can be a powerful ritual.

SO MUCH HAPPINESS

by Naomi Shihab Nye

It is difficult to know what to do with so much happiness
With sadness there is something to rub against,
a wound to tend with lotion and cloth.
When the world falls in around you, you have pieces to pick up,
something to hold in your hands, like ticket stubs or change.

But happiness floats.
It doesn't need you to hold it down.
It doesn't need anything.
Happiness lands on the roof of the next house, singing,
and disappears when it wants to.
You are happy either way.
Even the fact that you once lived in a peaceful tree house
and now live over a quarry of noise and dust
cannot make you unhappy.
Everything has a life of its own,
it too could wake up filled with possibilities
of coffee cake and ripe peaches,
and love even the floor which needs to be swept,
the soiled linens and scratched records........

Since there is no place large enough
to contain so much happiness,
you shrug, you raise your hands, and it flows out of you
into everything you touch. You are not responsible.
You take no credit, as the night takes no credit
for the moon, but continues to hold it, and share it,
and in that way, be known.

SECTION TWO

Pathways to a Deeper Connection With Our Authentic Self

What are the *actual* working dynamics of living from the Authentic Self? Section Two addresses this question by presenting a wide range of pathways, principles and tools that I have found to be essential. It also demonstrates how to use each of them in our day-to-day lives.

"We each have a spiritual current that runs through our lives—a river.
Connected to that current, our work, our life, has power.
I constantly ask myself: What is my relationship to that current?
Am I letting it guide me or am I forcing my will upon my life?
It is so easy to lose touch with that current.
When I am connected, my life has a flow.
The most amazing things happen.
Help comes my way, I meet "fellow travelers," people whose
energy supports mine, and we both come away reinforced.
Doors open. Bills get paid.
Being in touch with the spiritual current means first
being able to listen to oneself, being in sync with oneself."

~ Roderick MacIver

CHAPTER 4

Awakening to Spirit

"Love will take care of you.
Love is the guiding Light inside of you.
Pure love is the Soul."

~ John-Roger

GAVIN'S GRADUATION & AWAKENING

Ashamed and scared. That's how I felt as I walked onto the stage to receive my diploma after completing my master's degree program in Counseling & Guidance. I was 25 years old and my long-held goal had been to become a licensed therapist and start my own private practice. However, when graduation day arrived, I felt wildly unprepared with the knowledge, skillset and confidence to counsel other people on a professional basis.

As was common in the field of psychology, our degree program was solely academic and theoretical. We primarily studied and discussed different modes of psychotherapy, and were provided little opportunity to engage directly in the therapeutic process. On top of that, none of the classes supported students in identifying and healing their own unresolved psychological issues, of which I certainly had my share.

"Now what?" was the thought that ran through my mind as I stared at the diploma in my hand. I looked over at my mom in the audience. She was beaming with pride. I was

confused and lost. I secretly thought something was wrong with me and was not sure where to turn next. Something in me knew there was a missing ingredient, though I was completely unaware of what it was.

That "missing ingredient" showed up a few months afterwards, when a good friend invited me to an open house for a yoga teacher training program. At the time, I knew nothing of religion or spirituality or the difference between the two. Amazingly, my master's degree studies in psychology did not include any mention of spirituality. In addition, our family was not religious in any way when I was growing up. I had only seen ministers on television or heard them on the radio and was turned off by how they always seemed to be trying to sell me something.

I encountered a distinctly different scenario at this gathering. People were attentive and sharing warmly with each other. The presence of love permeated the atmosphere. This experience felt foreign yet native at the same time. I was deeply drawn to this heartfelt way of engaging with other people.

One week later, I went to a party in the Pacific Palisades, and once again had the experience of being moved by the presence of the people there. They were relaxed, looking in each other's eyes, and being sincerely open and emotionally intimate with one another. I was in awe that at a casual weekend party I experienced a depth of closeness among others that I had never felt throughout my University studies. This is what I had been searching for. The overwhelming feeling of love in that room brought me to tears.

These new friends were graduates of transformational workshops offered by an organization called Insight Seminars. The following week, I had the opportunity to participate in their initial 5-day program, The Awakening Heart. I was astonished at how emotionally safe I felt in that room. On the second day of this experiential workshop, I broke down and cried uncontrollably in front of the group. So many layers of the pain that I'd buried throughout my teens were finally given a safe place to emerge and be met. Although I was somewhat embarrassed having shared such depth of emotion in a room filled with strangers, many participants approached me with tenderness and affirming words for my courage and vulnerability. Amazingly, I felt truly seen and honored as a strong, sensitive man who was on a journey of healing and awakening. In that beautiful, caring atmosphere over 5 days, over and over I touched into my true nature. I recognized in an undeniable way that I carried within myself profound love, compassion and wisdom. I also saw the same was true for everyone else.

This flow of revelations sparked my conscious relationship with the presence of a loving Spirit, and thankfully I felt no need to get caught up in my mind with what to call it. I was being welcomed into an invisible dimension of unconditional love. In the most natural of ways,

I felt reunited with the presence of Light inside of me that I'd begun losing touch with when I was 10 years old and our family's traumas began. I was returning home…

THE NATURE OF EMERGING TRUTH

When Yo-Yo Ma, the master cellist, performs, there's a truth he is transmitting through his instrument that touches all present in profound ways. Truth is an energetic frequency that each of us can feel and recognize whenever we encounter it. Thankfully, my life was beginning to open in powerful new ways as I dared to express my depth and truth.

I saw a video years ago in which the performing artist Kenny Loggins described his experience of playing his music for dolphins. When he was in a groove with his guitar, they came close to him and hung around. And when he wasn't, the dolphins wandered elsewhere. Our connection with authenticity and the flow of Spirit is innate, which is perhaps why animals and young children cannot easily be fooled.

As you listen to your own truth, you are more attuned to the distinctive language of your Authentic Self. You can learn about its particular cues and signals by asking yourself questions like, "What does my body feel like when inspired ideas come to me?" and, "In what ways can I open to receive a flow of inspiration?" and, "How can I distinguish truth from falseness?"

When walking through challenging life passages, it can be a struggle to discern the truest course of action. You can get caught in the doubts and fears of your mind and feel paralyzed. It is crucial to realize that your inner truth *will* continue to reveal itself to you as you keep moving forward. When you're moving in a new direction and taking action steps, no matter how small, it's essential to pay close attention to your internal compass to assure that the course you are on is aligned with your Authentic Self. A willingness to adjust course along the way is a powerful strategy.

Years ago I learned that Apollo 11, the American spaceflight that first landed humans on the Moon in 1969, was actually off-course 98% of the time throughout its journey in space. Making continual course-corrections was its key to success.

"God can't steer a parked car!"
~ Unknown

Fortunately, the more you practice relying upon your inner knowing—your True Self's guidance—the more trusting you become in reading your body's subtle ways of communicating its wisdom.

Invitation for Discovery

I invite you to take a moment to consider the action steps you are currently taking to move forward with a project or relationship in your life? Are you receiving inner communications that indicate you are—or are not—on the right course? In what specific ways are you experiencing this feedback? Perhaps it is a fleeting feeling, or perhaps it is a deeper intuition. Observe how outer circumstances are—or are not—aligning and cooperating with your inner truth as you are moving forward. Capture notes in your *Journal* of any new awarenesses you're discovering.

MICHAEL AWAKENS

When I was 25, my brother Michael's life trajectory as a hardened criminal seemed to have taken a dramatic turn. He had just turned 30 and was still behind bars, this time in Oregon for armed robbery. He wrote me and my parents, informing us that something powerful had happened to him. He had turned his life over to Jesus Christ. He made a request that we visit him in prison so he could share more with us. I immediately suspected this was a ploy to manipulate his way out of prison. I feared that my parents would be victimized by his deception. My mom and dad were also apprehensive. However, despite our skepticism, we booked a flight to see him.

Once again, we found ourselves entering another federal penitentiary. I felt the familiar feeling of claustrophobia as soon as we drove into the parking lot. Right away I couldn't breathe. By now I had visited upwards of a dozen of these places, and the color of the walls was always drab. I again felt the menacing presence of rival gang members silently staring at us as we walked through a fenced corridor next to the prison yard.

I still jumped every time the heavy metal doors clanged behind us as we made our way to the prisoner visiting room. We sat on edge as we waited for Michael to be led into the room across from us.

As we did, a door opened and a prisoner was guided into the room. Only one guard accompanied him. It looked like they were casually talking, and both appeared calm. Was this my brother? He no longer had a beard or long hair. His eyes were different. He was pleasant and friendly as he sat down in the room across from us, surprisingly unshackled.

As Michael began sharing with us, we were stunned. It was undeniable. We were witnessing a genuinely transformed man. My angry, violent, hateful white-supremacist brother was no more. The façade had been dropped. He was sincerely repentant, kind and engaging. For the first time in years, he was earnestly asking us questions about our own lives. His whole countenance had changed, and it was as if I had an entirely different brother. I had never met this humble and genuine man before, not even when I was a child. Was this a dream? His face and eyes were glowing—his inner Light was now shining.

He shared with us that he had finally grasped the hopelessness of his destructive path. A deep longing for more had grown in him, and one day he had opened his heart to hear what a prison ministry volunteer had to offer. As he did, something stirred inside him, and a profoundly loving Presence washed over his entire being. Within minutes, he had surrendered himself to a life-changing relationship with Jesus Christ. We were stunned, of course, and did our best to welcome this new Michael into our hearts and our lives. It was a miracle, an absolute miracle.

THE OPENING HEART

At a certain point in our life journey, many of us begin consciously searching for greater meaning. Our attention is drawn deeper, beneath the surface of our life, to discover how to live with greater fulfillment. We carry a longing to unfasten ourselves from the ways of our adapted self and respond to the hidden potentials that our Authentic Self has been hinting to us at all along.

When we are ready, the human heart recognizes the presence of love and truth. Michael and I both came into a season of our lives in which we recognized Spirit and surrendered to it, each in our own way. Ironically, our respective processes of awakening occurred around the same time. True spirituality transcends all separation, including decades of racism and hatred. As human beings open to the experience of Divine love, we realize that we are not alone, that we are connected. The spiritual journey is an evolutionary process which continually requires that we move beyond previously established boundaries. It involves sincerely opening to a profound relationship with the Invisible.

Ever since kindergarten, I had been curious about what made the chicks in that incubator start to peck their way out of their shells. Later in my life, I discovered an astounding fact: at a certain point in the unhatched chick's gestation, a poisonous gas is emitted from inside the shell—which means that they actually *have* to peck their way out in order to survive. Having finally faced enough of our own pain, Michael and I had each successfully broken free from our protective shells into our new lives.

Invitation for Discovery

As you reflect upon your life journey, I invite you to identify a groundbreaking time in your life in which you broke free from the "shells" that had previously bound you. What life circumstances unfolded at that time that may have catalyzed your awakening? Capture in your *Journal* as many specifics as you can remember about this liberating experience, including identifying the specific qualities and expressions that newly emerged from within you. Consider the common pattern of how the shell may not have been sensed by you until it began to crack.

SPIRIT BECOMES MY PARTNER

Through my involvement with Insight trainings, I learned about the University of Santa Monica (USM) and their Master's Degree program in Spiritual Psychology. This program offered a transformational approach to both personal healing and in-depth training as a counselor. I enrolled immediately. As the spiritual dimension continued to take its central, unifying place in my understanding and experience of life, my world continued to transform.

One day in class at USM, it was my turn to counsel a fellow student working on one of her real-life issues. Our session was being observed by the rest of the class. Although I was initially quite nervous given many eyes were watching us, I soon became aware of a deeper presence and inner knowing guiding me. Throughout the session, I held immense respect for this older woman who sat in front of me and felt a gift of confidence and intuition flow through me. Though her life experiences were very different from my own, her Authentic Self was deeply familiar to me. I knew it held the answers she was seeking. The world around us seemed to disappear and time stood still for almost an hour as we worked together to heal one of her core limiting life patterns. Compassion and love were present throughout the session, and I experienced the unmistakable presence of Spirit flowing through me.

When we were complete and turned to face the others, having forgotten that they were even in the room, everyone was in tears. The class facilitator and each student provided rich, affirming feedback about the depth of my love and effectiveness of my counseling skills. With my own direct experience of the session, combined with these empowering reflections, my heart received profound confirmation that counseling others in their healing and awakening was how I was going to serve the world. The incorporation of the spiritual dimension at the heart of my experience had changed everything. This realization brought with it an abiding sense of comfort, completeness and belonging. Not only had I finally found a true calling in my life, but Spirit was my faithful partner in its unfolding.

Shortly after this experience I was invited to join the USM faculty and began co-facilitating weekend classes for the University's Master's Degree program in Spiritual Psychology.

> *"The expression of your gifts may feel magical. It may feel like a gift that you received from somewhere else, but in truth it isn't. It is just you, the you that is usually obscured by the personality—the ego mind. Our gifts are our essence revealed."*
>
> ~ Unknown

MICHAEL'S IMPENDING RELEASE

Following his spiritual transformation, Michael became a model prisoner and, by everyone's account, was no longer deemed a threat to society. Despite his long history of violent crimes, the parole board in California scheduled him for an early release. As he had been one of the leaders of the Aryan Brotherhood, with first-hand knowledge of their darkest secrets and crimes, my parents and I were terrified for his safety. Would he make it out of prison alive?

Thankfully, a few months later, Michael let us know that his former gang members had decided not to kill him. It was clear to them that his transformation was authentic, and that he had no intention of becoming a stool pigeon.

EMBRACING OUR TRUTH

Human life, as our DNA and fingerprints imply, expresses itself through the uniqueness of individuals. Each of us has a distinctive way of seeing and being. To embrace and live from our truth means to express ourself in authentic ways. We have the direct responsibility to pay close attention to our experience and determine what is true for us. Thankfully, we have been provided with an internal compass, an intuitive instrument that guides us, a consciousness of knowing.

The answers for how to recognize and live in accordance with your deepest nature cannot be found outside yourself. There are no universal formulas or series of prescribed steps to support you in awakening. The process of discerning your internal truth is highly personal, and is actually learned best through trial and error. Wise discernment is the natural result of seeing through the lens of Love, and only you can discern what is authentic for you.

MY RELATIONSHIP WITH THE DIVINE

In my late 20's, I continued to immerse myself in spiritual and psychological workshops. In addition to my role with the University faculty, I made Spirit more of a reality in my daily life, continually making myself available to its presence. I initiated a daily meditation practice as part of a nourishing morning ritual. Chanting and singing out loud consistently opened my heart energies.

I welcomed a relationship with a profoundly loving spiritual teacher, and thankfully he taught me, early on, the importance of not falling into the trap of worshipping a teacher. He said, "Don't let me get in the way of your relationship with the Divine." Having the benefit of a wise and experienced spiritual traveler was invaluable in strengthening my own direct, conscious connection with Spirit.

My growing reservoir of love gave me greater permission and strength to be introspective and honest in confronting the many conditioned layers of my false self. I found that the simple act of lovingly acknowledging them started a process of dismantling and dissolving them. I became more and more skillful at noticing when I was starting to get upset and could gently turn the tide by taking conscious breaths and calming down.

I realized that wherever I was, whatever I was doing, I could lead an uplifted spiritual life. It's not about meditating properly or being with the right group of people. It's not about the clothes we wear or our diet, the shape of our body or where we live or work. It's not about what church or temple we belong to or how often we attend. I began to see that we are each a temple, a place of worship—blessed beyond measure.

"There will soon be no more priests.
Their work is done.
Every man shall be his own priest."
~ Walt Whitman

SELF-IMAGE VS. AUTHENTICITY

When we talk in our culture about authenticity, about being true to ourselves, we're often mistakenly referring to being true to a mental image we are carrying, a pre-conceived idea of ourselves and the kind of person we think we should be. For instance, "I'm a good person, and a good person is always loving, responsible, and giving to others," or, "I'm really pissed off about how my partner treated me this morning, but I'm spiritual and I shouldn't get angry."

When it comes to connecting with your deeper truth, it's essential to recognize the distinction between your ego's self-image and your true authentic expression. You are not your thoughts, nor are you the "shoulds" you hold about yourself. Your self-concepts are comprised of mental images that tend to imprison you, while your authenticity is a vibrant presence that continually reflects and refreshes your humanity and divinity.

As you journey along your path, you can steadily identify and let go of any misconceptions about what it means to be "spiritual." What you are really seeking is to let go of the defenses and pretenses through which you've endeavored to protect what is most precious within you. The fundamental principle is that there is nothing you need to do to be spiritual—you already are. And, your colorful and sometimes turbulent emotional landscape is not an impediment to that. It's part of what it means to be "a spiritual being having a human experience."

Invitation for Discovery

I invite you to take a moment to reflect upon whether you have any specific mental concepts about what it means for you to be spiritual. Do you have any fixed notions about what this should look like? Next, make a conscious choice to set aside this self-image—your story about the kind of person you are or are not. You will discover that without your story, you don't disappear. Instead, the real beauty that you possess on a deeper level actually emerges. Capture any revelations in your *Journal.*

WHAT IS YOUR TRUTH?

by John Lee

What is your truth?
Ask your heart, your back,
your bones, and your dreams.
Listen to that truth with your whole body.
Understand that this truth will destroy no one
and that you're too old to be sent to your room.
Move into your truth as though it were an old house.
Walk through each room.
See, hear, and feel what it is to live there.
Try to love what you find, and remember
the words that come to you as you explore.
You won't land in a world made to order;
some people in your life may
not like what you discover.
But those who remain will be allies,
people who breathe deeply and listen.

CHAPTER 5

The Art of Self-Observation

"The highest spiritual practice is
Self-observation without judgment."

~ Swami Kripalu

OUR INNER WORLD

Our inner world is our true source of reality and power. The flow and fulfillment of a truly successful outer life is built upon a vibrant inner life. Without this core relationship, material success can certainly be achieved, but it will never bring the deep fulfillment we are seeking.

The biggest obstacle in our relationship with our Authentic Self is any distortions in our thinking. Most of us have handed over the reins of our inner authority to our habitual fears, doubts and addiction to the negative emotions that accompany them. The false self takes charge of our life early on, when we are under the stress of trauma, and have not yet consciously reawakened to the abundant source of energy that is the Authentic Self.

The mind often convinces us that we should be different or somehow be other than where we are right now. This is a fantasy. Learning to move past our judgments and limiting stories into greater neutrality is a vital skill. This is Self-observation, the golden road to higher awareness and a peaceful inner life.

SELF-OBSERVATION

Self-observation is a state of active, moment-to-moment awareness of our thoughts, feelings, bodily sensations and surrounding environment. We all have this innate ability to observe ourselves. It is a practice of witnessing the flow of our experience as it unfolds, through the gentle lens of acceptance, without judging it as right or wrong, good or bad. Bringing the non-judgmental attention of our Authentic Self to the present moment opens us to greater Self-understanding. By choosing to be aware and allowing ourselves to acknowledge the presence of love, the grip that our past has had on us steadily loosens and no longer dictates our present and future.

Thus, being aware of being aware is a human birthright. The evolution towards living more authentically involves bringing what has previously been unconscious into your conscious awareness—so you are no longer living on automatic pilot. The limiting patterns of your false self can only retain their powerful hold on you when you remain unconscious to them. Expanding awareness brings freedom and grants you an opportunity to make wiser choices.

Self-observation can be a powerful avenue for releasing patterns of thought and emotions that cause problems in your personal and professional relationships. Rather than dwelling on the past or anxiously speculating about the future, through Self-observation you can participate in your relationships from the vantage point of the present.

WHO IS THE ONE OBSERVING?

Once you embark upon a path of higher awareness, the internal process of observation awakens. As it does so, a common question emerges: "Who is the one watching?" and, "Who is in charge of my consciousness?" The answer to both questions is the same: the real you, your Authentic Self. It is both a state of awareness and the natural leader of your inner world, the one who witnesses and accepts all aspects of yourself. It doesn't take sides, it facilitates open communication and its focus is building unity.

The Authentic Self resides at your center—in your heart—and is often felt as a sense of well-being, contentment and joy. You recognize it as good-natured and free of irritation. This doesn't mean that it avoids confrontation when it is appropriate, it just means there is a graciousness about how you navigate turbulent storms when the Authentic Self is at the helm.

Self-observation is analogous to sitting alone in a movie theatre, watching a movie about your life playing on the screen. You are seeing and feeling your journey unfold with all its joys, pains, victories and setbacks. As you experience your ups and downs, you are simultaneously practicing the skill of remembering to come back to yourself—not as the actor on the screen, but as the compassionate observer seated in the audience.

The aim of Self-observation is not to quiet your mind and emotions, or attempt to achieve a state of eternal calm. The goal is to simply pay attention to the present moment—no matter how intense or turbulent it may be. Your mind has a tendency to incessantly create thoughts, judgments and stories. When it does, you can choose to observe them. The invitation is to return, again and again, to the present moment as a neutral observer. There is no need to judge yourself for whatever thoughts flow in and out of your awareness. You are not responsible for what comes into your consciousness, only for what you hold there and act upon. You can be compassionate with your wandering mind and know that this is just something all human minds do. You can gently speak to your mind, letting it know with compassionate reassurance that you are in charge and inviting it to follow your lead.

Merely witnessing what is unfolding in uncomfortable situations allows you to look at circumstances from a different perspective. For instance, when you feel awkward, your initial reaction might be to avoid the situation that appears to be making you uncomfortable—or else jump in and try to do something that will alleviate your anxiety. Maybe you blurt out your opinion or try to "fix" the situation. However, learning to participate in your experience without the need to take impulsive action is a strategy that invites an experience of ease and grace.

Witnessing is not a passive process. By spaciously observing in a way that reflects a degree of detachment from a specific outcome, you remain more neutral and grounded. As your mind gets quieter, you'll receive spontaneous insights from deeper within you about the real nature of the situation, which enables you to take effective rather than impulsive action.

As you proceed with your day, invite yourself to practice the skill of staying present through Self-observation. One of the best ways to return to the present moment is by bringing your awareness to your rising and falling breath. Taking a few minutes to gently and deeply breath in and out can return you to center and naturally quiet your mind. Tuning into your flow of breathing and sensations in your body helps bring you into the here and now.

SELF-REMEMBERING

G.I. Gurdjieff, a 19th-century mystic and philosopher, taught his students a unique tool for remaining conscious of their deeper Self during the stresses of their day-to-day lives. He introduced them to a powerful yet remarkably simple exercise called Self-remembering.

Gurdjieff invited them to continually repeat, silently throughout the day, the sentence, "I am the one who..." and each time completing the sentence with a description of their awareness at that particular moment. For example, "I am the one who...is listening to my own voice. I am the one who...is sipping a cup of coffee. I am the one who...feels anxious in my belly." Each sentence starts anew with "I am"—a universal name for the Soul, the Divine, the Authentic Self.

Each time you complete a statement of your present awareness, you avoid grabbing onto and getting caught in its story—you simply move on by repeating the sentence again, "I am the one who..." Each time, you complete the sentence anew with whatever new awareness is emerging for you at that moment. By repeating this process, like a mantra, you continually move deeper into greater connection with your authenticity. You are less engaged with the mind and its desire to be involved in stories. Gurdjieff recognized that the Authentic Self is the sacred witness of all that's unfolding in one's consciousness.

Self-remembering is a spiritual practice that allows you to recognize whatever you are experiencing in your flow of awareness, to embrace and express it, and then move on. This practice can be done silently or out loud. Many find that writing out this process can also serve to amplify its powerful impact.

"Without Self-knowledge, man cannot be free, he cannot govern himself and he will always remain a slave."

~ G.I. Gurdjieff

As your mind relaxes in a flow of observation without judgment, you often gently enter into a state of equanimity. Then, your body also relaxes and moves into new levels of peace. This process also works in the other direction—as you still your body, the flow of your mind relaxes. In this spaciousness afforded by the practice of Self-remembering, you will find that you are less stressed and better able to engage in a graceful way with the people and events in your life.

Invitation for Discovery

The next time you find yourself feeling out of balance, or perhaps not aware of what you are experiencing inside, I invite you to set in motion the Self-remembering process by repeating, "I am the one who..." and complete the sentence with whatever is present for you. Remember that this can be done inwardly, out loud, or through writing, whichever way is most supportive for you. As you do this, imagine that the thoughts and feelings flowing through you are pictures on a movie screen. Instead of analyzing them or getting hooked into telling yourself a story about them, simply observe them moment to moment as they flow by. Capture your reflections in your *Journal*.

SACRED WITNESS

"Everything is sacred" is a core principle of Celtic spirituality. From this oneness perspective, a rock is as sacred as a Soul. Consciously recognizing the sacred in everything is a spiritual practice in itself, yet it is not something you can do with your mind. In fact, if you attempt to do it mentally or mechanically, the beautiful healing this practice can provide will elude you.

Start by focusing on the love you feel in your heart that arises when you call to mind someone or something that is precious to you. When you slow yourself down and allow your focus to move from your mind to your heart, you begin to see through eyes that are filled with love and appreciation. More and more, you become aware of the universal, sacred energy in everything—the unfathomable preciousness of life.

As you walk through your day, you can consciously practice being a sacred witness to all things in life. You can summon an embracing field of awareness that observes without judging. Then, when you're doing something as simple as putting on your socks, you may recognize that even your socks are made up of universal energy, and therefore they are sacred. Rooted in your breath, you consciously witness yourself putting on your socks rather than doing it automatically. You may feel gladness in your heart for the warmth of the socks, for the people who helped design and make them, and for your good fortune to have them clean, handy and ready to wear.

Similarly, when you're hungry, you can recognize that your hunger is also sacred, for without it, you would not be impelled to seek the nourishment you need to survive. As you mature in your practice of witnessing the sacred, you will experience the healing presence of the universal energy of the Divine, which is the essence of your Authentic Self. This is who you truly are. You are forever innocent, curious and eager to learn more. This dynamic presence is always radiating from within you, and your connection to it is fueled by simple awareness.

Invitation for Discovery

While you are continuing to go about your normal activities, I invite you to take 15 minutes to consciously practice being a sacred witness. During this time, you are intentionally heightening your recognition of the sacred energy in everything you encounter inwardly and outwardly. As you can easily forget your commitment to this practice, it may be supportive to set up a timer to remind yourself to continue to hold this focus. If this exercise proves meaningful to you, you can take even longer periods of time to engage this practice. You could expand it to 30 minutes and then more. You may find that this actually becomes a very natural process. You can capture in your *Journal* any new discoveries about how this conscious practice impacts the quality of your day-to-day experience.

BALANCING LOVE & TRUTH

When you are being true to who you are, you may notice that your expression to others will carry an equal blend of love and truth. If you bring forward too much love and not enough truth when communicating, you may find that you are too soft in your energy or hesitant to express honestly and courageously. Conversely, if you lock in on the truth with others and pursue it devoid of love, your expression may be received by them as arrogant, harsh or cool.

As you build a conscious relationship with your Authentic Self, you will learn to be intimate with others with equal levels of love and truth. Genuine empowerment is when your knowing Self, which naturally carries this balance, begins to take charge of your life. As this happens, a surprising sense of peace emerges and previously unknown inner resources reveal themselves.

"To be yourself in a world that is constantly trying to make you something else is the greatest accomplishment."

~ Ralph Waldo Emerson

FACING REALITY

Most of us have had the experience of being afraid of sharing our truth with someone else because we sense it might not be well received. In much the same way, we may find it challenging to handle a truth someone shares with us. This might be a small truth, such as not wanting to hear that our car needs repairs because we can't afford them. Or, it could be an enormous truth, such as voicing that the marriage we are in may be in far greater trouble than we had recognized. Usually, such a truth is right there for us to see, but as humans we've developed elaborate ways of hiding it from ourselves.

We avoid the truth because it scares us and evokes unpleasant feelings, or because we simply don't know what to do with it. We create our life based on a particular understanding or sense of ourselves, and it takes a strong and resilient person to make peace with the reality that we may have grown and changed in ways that necessitate reconfiguring our circumstances. It is hard to resist the temptation to attempt to avoid hurting the other person—or our entrenched sense of identity—by moving into denial. However, we can only avoid the truth in our heart for so long before it makes itself known in more insistent and painful ways.

This is what transpired in my relationship with Zena. As much as we loved each other, my deeper truth made it clear that the emerging importance of spirituality in my life journey was incompatible with her life choices at that time. As difficult as it was to accept, my Authentic Self guided me to honorably bring our romantic relationship to a close.

Ultimately, no matter how painful it is, you are well served by letting down your defenses and opening your eyes to the new reality that is emerging. Sometimes sharing our truth with another can be like a quick "pulling off of a band-aid," and other times we are guided to employ a more incremental sharing of our truth to account for a tremendous shift that is taking place in our lives. Whatever your process is, when you face the truth and accept that you may have to adjust your life to accommodate it, you come into greater alignment with your Authentic Self. And, as you realize how painful it can be to acknowledge your own truth, you become more compassionate and supportive of those around you as they too are challenged with finding the courage to face their own truth.

WITH THAT MOON LANGUAGE

by Hafiz

Admit something.
Everyone you see, you say to them, "Love me."
Of course you do not do this out loud, otherwise
Someone would call the cops.
Still though, think about this, this great pull in us to connect.
Why not become the one who lives
With a full moon in each eye that is always saying
With that sweet moon language
What every other eye
In this world
Is dying to hear?

CHAPTER 6

Divine Sovereignty: Owning Our Soul's Curriculum

"Spiritual progression is a continual process of leaving behind the old, familiar patterns and venturing into the new."

~ John-Roger

MICHAEL COMES CLEAN

"I am writing to confess to a murder." Michael wrote these words in a letter to authorities in 1982.

A year earlier, he had been safely paroled from prison for good behavior. He moved to a small town in Oregon and become an active member of a local church. The entire congregation embraced Michael, helped him find a job as well as enroll at a local college.

Despite his life-changing spiritual breakthrough—or perhaps because of it—Michael was struggling with his conscience. The focal point of his gnawing guilt was a 15-day crime spree in California and Oregon that had occurred 6 years before his religious conversion. His rampage included the cold-blooded murder of an 18-year old black teenager, which had remained an unsolved crime.

Michael was committed to the purification of his inner life. His connection with Christ meant everything to him. After months of agonizing reflection, and with the support and encouragement of his newfound spiritual family, he finally decided to fully confess to his crimes. In the spirit of atonement, he recognized that stepping forward and speaking his truth was his only genuine course of action. This confession was astonishing, particularly because he knew this meant that he would be going back to prison. As part of his healing path, he was willing to face the consequences of his actions.

Thus, he sent a written confession to the San Mateo County District Attorney's office, providing the horrific details of driving through Redwood City, California on Highway 101, when he saw a young black man driving. He did not know who the man was—all that mattered was the color of his skin. That was enough for him to pull out a shotgun and kill him. At the time, he had been drifting along the West Coast with other members of the Aryan Brotherhood. He noted that he had been trying to impress them and gain status within the gang.

In response to his letter, Michael was arrested and brought back to California. The Redwood City police detective who transported him across state lines was so moved by the purity of Michael's heart that he testified to the judge on his behalf as a character witness. Michael was indeed convicted and sent back to prison, yet for a shortened sentence due to his confession and exemplary behavior.

"Speaking our truth is the most powerful tool we all have."

~ Oprah Winfrey

STEPPING PAST OUR FALSE SELF

Michael's path is a dramatic tale of 2 lives...and 2 selves. For most of his adult life, my brother was dominated by his false self. He was so disconnected from his deeper nature that he chose to commit murder on a whim. Underneath his rage lived a deeply sensitive, profoundly wounded human being. Once Michael freed himself from the shackles of his false self and began living from his Authentic Self, a brand new life commenced. He never harmed anyone again.

Our mind frequently masquerades as the keeper of truth and loves to portray itself as our authority. It can get lost as it pretends to know, attempting to persuade us and others into believing that something is true when it is not. The false voice in our mind is not a truth-teller. It is an inner critic that repeatedly echoes false beliefs it developed from traumatic experiences in our childhood. We often tend to believe that we are what we think, thus unwittingly constrict ourselves to an existence bound by limited thoughts that are rooted in trauma.

We see this same dynamic play itself out among public figures who have lost their connection with their own truth and speak in ways that only further their ambitions. We also witness their public fall from grace if their lies are finally exposed and they are held accountable. My brother was trapped in his own web of violent and destructive illusions, until a spiritual awakening enabled him to reconnect with his compassionate heart.

Regardless of how lost we may feel, at some point we catch a glimpse of our Authentic Self and seek reunion. That's when we become willing to do whatever it takes to step free and live a more joyful and fulfilling life.

When we awaken, like Michael, to the realization that we have been living a lie, we recognize that the only remedy is the strong medicine of truth. When we are willing to face the reality of our current life circumstances, the wise Self, which has been hidden within, can rise to the occasion. And that's how it was for Michael, who chose with his confession to surrender his outer freedom for the inner freedom that only his deeper truth provided.

During times of challenge, we have the opportunity to seek liberation from self-deception, and when we do, new reservoirs of inner strength become available to us. The True Self, the one that steadily whispers to us with a kind, affirming presence, delivers its message with quiet confidence. As we maintain our connection to this presence of truth, and have the courage to act from it, we become more relaxed in our body and our outer communications radiate with the loving certainty of this voice.

While each of us has a unique path, at the heart of every Soul's curriculum is learning to love. We all have the opportunity to steadily set aside the ways of our false self, to live from the presence of our Authentic Self and create the lives we truly desire.

GAVIN'S CALLING UNFOLDS

It was 1983 and I had just completed the program at USM. Following my realizations about my life's calling and while maintaining my teaching responsibilities at USM, I finally felt well-prepared to move forward and establish my private counseling practice. I had learned a multitude of self-healing tools to facilitate my deeper transformation and had had many opportunities to use these tools to help others in their self-healing work. Working out of my home office in Sherman Oaks, California, a steady stream of clients flowed my way. I also designed and facilitated my own transformational workshops, and they were well received.

To the outsider, it may have appeared that my life was now perfectly in place. Although by then I had indeed begun building greater levels of psychological and spiritual stability, I was still battling feelings of unworthiness and memories from my dark teenage years. Cycles of depression were still part of my inner landscape. Thankfully, I was beginning to recognize that mature spirituality involved having the courage to remain in close touch with my humanness and vulnerability—rather than some kind of romanticized escape from the reality of life's up and downs.

MICHAEL'S MINISTRY

Michael embraced his deeper truth and the power of love and became a source of wisdom and liberation for many others. After being released from prison for the last time, my brother moved back to Oregon. He resumed his dedication to serving his church community. Within a couple of years, he got married and became a respected elder in the church. While still covered with tattoos—though now neatly groomed, clothed and mild-mannered—Michael was a trusted mentor to the hundreds of teens in the large congregation. He spoke of his experiences, his pain and remorse, and ultimately his life-transforming revelations about the inhumanity of racism that he had gained through spiritual insight. As they listened to his message, the teens were inspired to embrace the strength and tenderness within their own hearts.

CATHY'S HEALING

The spirit of transformation spread throughout my entire family. My sister, Cathy, triumphantly recovered from 17 years of heroin addiction with the steady support of Narcotics

Anonymous (NA). Those who engage in serious drug-use in their early teens and become long-term addicts are rarely able to sustain successful recovery and live fulfilling lives. Cathy defied the odds. Eventually she and her daughter moved to Oregon and joined the same church community as my brother. Michael and Cathy rekindled their bond from their earliest years, and their lives intertwined with deeper meaning and purpose as they both immersed themselves in lives of devotion and service.

MOM & DAD'S JOURNEY

Like me, my parents were still reeling from the years of emotional trauma within our family. Seeing the benefits I received from my immersion in psychology and spirituality, amazingly my mom entered into therapy and began realizing how many wounds she had been carrying. My parents, who had never done any personal growth work, and who had no idea who spiritual teachers like Alan Watts or Ram Dass were, suddenly started attending transformational workshops, including some that I facilitated. I recognized the rarity of their willingness as parents to wholeheartedly participate and evolve in a conscious way. My dad's inner work became an integral part of his continued remission from cancer. My parents and I meditated together. It was so refreshing to witness such salt-of-the-earth people savoring new levels of coming alive. It was as if we were from the same tribe, and our shared transformational journey brought each of us indescribable levels of healing within our family.

DIVINE SOVEREIGNTY

Sovereignty is the domain of the Authentic Self, and is defined as owning our inherent inner authority and nobility. Most people are not aware of this consciousness of sovereignty or how to access it. However, if we are to lead an authentic life, it is essential that we learn. Learning to tune in and live from our sovereignty inspires others to do the same.

While our family had limited control of what happened in our outer environment, we each in our own way learned to take some degree of stewardship of our internal environment. This enabled us to respond to what was taking place in and around us from a place of greater acceptance and empowerment.

While sovereignty resides in each of us, in subtle and not-so-subtle ways we often hand over the rulership of our consciousness to our false self or give our power away to others—hoping they can guide us to a better life. In doing so, we experience ourselves as victims of circumstances and ignore the vast resources that lie within us. Fortunately, it doesn't have to be this way. We can choose a new paradigm.

Sovereignty is the cornerstone of conscious authenticity, of stepping past being run by our unconscious choices as we embrace our hero's journey. It is experienced as a palpable sense of knowing your own inherent beauty and divinity—which comes from an expanded awareness that is accessible through our hearts. When you rest in this place of heart-centered sovereignty and are faced with important life decisions, you can both ask for and receive Spirit's guidance and follow its lead.

Sovereignty requires that our Authentic Self remain in dynamic and intimate relationship with all the dimensions of our consciousness, including our Divine nature, mind, emotions, body and dreams. Someone navigating from within genuine sovereignty will first consult with any aspects in their consciousness that may have input about the current issue at hand. As it gathers these valuable perspectives, our Authentic Self attunes to the most aligned choices that are congruent with our highest intentions. This is the unifying power of sovereignty.

With so much on the line, my brother's willingness to honor his own Soul's curriculum by acting upon his inner directive and confess to murder, was a powerful demonstration of exercising Divine sovereignty. At a most critical crossroad in his life, no matter the outer cost, he chose the greatest freedom available—that which came from living in integrity with his deepest truth.

Invitation for Discovery

I welcome you to take a few minutes to close your eyes. Take a few deep breaths. Attuning inwardly, identify an area of your life that has been troubling you. Spend some time observing this aspect of your life through the eyes of your Authentic Self, the consciousness that is in contact with all your inner aspects. Simply observe and be with what you experience from this neutral, caring place within you. See if any inspiration naturally arises about how you might take greater sovereignty in this dimension of your life. How, specifically, might you recognize the core learnings that make up your own Soul's curriculum—and take charge in this situation by stepping into noble leadership? Remember, a tiny step is as noble as any. Capture notes about your unfolding process in your *Journal*.

SELF-HONORING

A hallmark of living from the Authentic Self is carrying a consciousness of Self-honoring. By honoring ourselves, by becoming our own most avid advocate and best friend, we anchor the quality of inner nobility.

Most of us have learned to seek this level of loving devotion from outside ourselves, whether it be from parents, a partner, children, friends or the public at large. It is easy to get caught in the trap of looking to a primary relationship—or a spiritual teacher—as our source of love and stability. Ultimately, this never works over the long term. This is not to say that we shouldn't welcome loving partnerships or wise mentoring, but externalizing our experience of love and power will not foster enduring sovereignty.

Truly, you are the one most capable of attuning to who you are, of learning to recognize and meet your deeper needs. You can still receive nourishment, guidance and support from others, as long as you recognize that your most sustainable strength and fulfillment is always sourced from within. It is all about being in touch with your inner roots, and understanding that living your greater inheritance in this world requires being connected with the vault of treasure within.

Honoring yourself as royalty is not egotistical. You are merely taking back the reins from the false self, who has been serving much like a regent who takes control of a country when the true ruler, the Authentic Self, has gone into hiding. Sovereignty doesn't make you more special than others, for we are all special. Stepping into sovereignty is rather an acknowledgment that everyone on the planet has an innate nobility and the capacity to exercise loving dominion within their consciousness. When we love ourselves so faithfully and tenderly, simply by our example we often inspire others to afford themselves the same luxury.

What greater privilege can you have, and how can you be of greater service to the world, than by taking responsibility for meeting your own physical, mental, emotional, financial and spiritual needs? In no way does this mean doing it all by yourself. Indeed, one of the touchstones of wise sovereignty is recognizing that you may not have all the answers, and thus your willingness to ask for support when it is needed is a sign of strength.

Invitation for Discovery

1. a) I invite you to identify a small but significant Self-honoring behavior that you could employ that would support you moving forward on one of the following levels: physical, mental, emotional or spiritual.

   b) Would you be willing to commit to consistently taking this loving action within the next week as a way that fosters a greater sense of Self-respect and trust?

2. a) I invite you to identify an arena in your life where you have felt in some way like a victim.

   b) In what specific ways has your false self been involved in this pattern?

   c) Identify a specific action you are willing to commit to that reflects taking sovereignty over this area of your life. Do this with a spirit of embracing this as an opportunity for learning and Self-support. In support of following through with your commitments, establish a gentle timeline for completion that spurs your motivation. Record the action steps and timeline in your *Journal*.

OUR UNIQUE VOICE

An ancient Irish folktale tells the story of a young boy who lived in a cottage on the shore of a large lake. He was curious about a particular flock of birds who lived in the trees on the lakeside directly across from his home. These birds were well known for the unique chorus of sounds they sang each morning. Their lovely, lilting cries traveled across the lake to him, and he came to love their beautiful sounds.

In his desire to have a closer relationship with the flock, he practiced imitating their call for weeks. Once he had it down perfectly, with great expectation, he called out to them one morning. He was, of course, hoping that the birds would recognize their own cry and respond. Alas, nothing happened. The birds ignored him and went about their own conversation. They made no response to his attempts to join them in their melodious songs. It was as if they didn't even know he existed. He tried again morning after morning to no avail. The boy was so disappointed that he finally gave up.

The next morning he had an insight: he wondered what would happen if he developed his own unique human call and sent this sound out across the lake to the birds. After working on his own cry for weeks, he finally discovered a sound that opened his heart and made him jubilant whenever he uttered it.

Early the next day, as soon as he voiced his unique signature call in the flock's direction, they immediately responded to him with a chorus of their beautiful singing. He was moved to tears. Enraptured by their conversation, from then on he and the birds shared in this nourishing ritual each morning.

WELCOMING SACRED COMMUNITY & MENTORS

As illustrated in this folktale, the human yearning for connection with what is natural and organic runs deep in our consciousness. If we are to successfully usher ourselves into an authentic life, consciously welcoming sacred community is of fundamental importance. The truth is, we flourish in sacred companionship, for this is where we can truly be seen and heard by those around us.

"We are human because of others."

~ Aristotle

A common pitfall when entering the arena of personal growth is thinking that we are alone in our struggles. Taking sovereign authority for our life includes the recognition that we all need outer support. Welcoming the gift and blessings of sacred community doesn't relinquish our dominion—it amplifies it.

We are not meant to heal and awaken on our own. In the evolving journey of each member of my family, a genuine and supportive community was a crucial ingredient in our respective transformations. Each of us found long-term, kindred communities that supported us in flourishing. My brother and sister found it within a traditional church community. My parents and I found it with the fellowship of like-hearted beings in a range of spiritual workshops and organizations.

"My soul yearns to discover individuals who can join me in exploring the Mystery of Life, who can do so without defense and with strength, vulnerability and a sense of inspiration."

~ Brugh Joy, M.D.

In essence, sacred community supports you in learning to be yourself, in recognizing and honoring your unique Soul's curriculum in this lifetime. It provides the possibility of doing together what is impossible to accomplish alone, of accessing the strength needed to risk making changes. Community provides a healing container to which you bring your authentic expression, and in witnessing each other unfold, all are empowered to continually know themselves more deeply.

"One does not make friends. One recognizes them."

~ Garth Henrichs

One form of sacred community is working closely over time with an aligned therapist or practitioner who is capable of holding sacred space for you as you navigate your healing and transformational journey. There can be tremendous leverage in giving yourself this gift.

Malidoma Patrice Some, an African transformational leader, outlined the essential characteristics of a truly healthy, sacred community:

❖ Sincere intention. It meets the intrinsic needs of every individual to both connect with the power within and be honored for their authentic nature.

❖ Unity of Spirit. The community feels an undivided sense of unity. Each member is like a cell in a body. The group needs the individual, and vice-versa.

❖ Trust. Everyone is moved to trust everyone else by principle. There is no sense of discrimination or elitism. This trust assumes that everyone is innately well-intentioned. (And trust is most available among those who are actively taking dominion over their own consciousness and behavior.)

❖ Openness. People are open to each other unreservedly. This means that individual problems quickly become community problems. Being open to each other depends on trust.

❖ Love and Caring. What you have is for everybody. There is a sense of sharing, which diminishes ego behavior and fosters a spirit of overflow.

❖ Home. It is not a place of distraction but a place of being. It is not a place where you reform, but a place you go home to.

Invitation for Discovery

1. I invite you to identify a potential source of sacred community—either a group or a one-on-one support person—that you might consider welcoming into your life to provide a greater sense of fellowship, support and growth.

2. What would be one specific step you could take to begin engaging in the avenue you've chosen? If you are experiencing

a call to action, I encourage you to take this step and check out whether this new source of community is genuinely nourishing for you. Being discerning about the sacred community you choose, including how you choose to participate within it, is essential. Note your responses and any next steps in your *Journal*.

THE GROUND OF BEING

by Gavin Frye

Out of the ground
are born all things.
The ground of being,
of inspiration,
of pain,
of ease.

Flow is our Divine right.
To know our own colors
is rapture.

Arise, allow the wind
to blow through your
branches and sing!

CHAPTER 7

Welcoming Change & Sacred Passages

"Soul is the source of change and the hidden connection between things. Through Soul, we connect to the most ancient knowledge—and to the most immediate aspects of our life."

~ Michael Meade

THE POWER OF CHANGE

As human beings, we continually find new ways to bring who we are into the world. Like the seed dropped from a tree onto the forest floor, we are instinctively drawn to grow and be a part of something larger than ourselves.

Just as the atmospheric conditions on our planet move through seasons, major change for human beings happens in cyclical patterns throughout our life. Change is inevitable, and always delivers hidden wisdom and profound gifts. Yet, unlike the rest of nature, we humans are the one strand of creation that can choose to resist our growth and blossoming. When our false self reacts defensively to life's stresses, it impedes us from pursuing our heart's passions. Alas, we can begin to forget what it means to be truly alive.

"Listen, are you breathing just a little and calling it a life?"

~ Mary Oliver

When things don't go the way we want in the world, we have a tendency to move into blame. Or, we take a stand that life just doesn't work for us. Placing blame is a misguided attempt to regain a sense of control. We unconsciously allow ourselves to create a false story of causality that rests on a paradigm of helplessness. The reality is that we are not in control of what happens outside of our own skin—and this is not a problem. Life happens according to its rules, not ours. Invariably, changes in our outer life become a catalyst which compel us to engage and expand with life just as it is.

"When you argue with reality, you lose, but only 100% of the time."

~ Byron Katie

WELCOMING THE UNKNOWN

Change requires a leap into the unknown. Often we have to feel like we are at the end of our rope before we are open to change and willing to take courageous action. When we feel stuck in our life, and seemingly unable to move forward, it is often because there is something about ourselves that we are not accepting. An essential step to facilitate change is to accept exactly where we are right now, whether or not we like it. Operating from greater cooperation with reality grants us the freedom to move beyond our old limits and make new choices.

Your Authentic Self has a perpetual yearning for meaning and truth, and possesses a childlike quality that is open and eager to embrace change. When young children are supported in trusting the freedom in their expression, they naturally expand and thrive. As you journey deeper into your truer nature, you can recognize yourself as a conscious creator and connect with your natural willingness to come more alive. In other words, awareness is the first step to change.

At key turning points in your life, major change begins with one simple change: moving your focus from the outer world to your inner world. This gives you greater access to receiving revelations from your deeper self.

In nature, the season of spring emerges from deep inside the earth and has its own timing and rhythm of transforming life. Like spring flowers mysteriously bursting up through the soil, real change is an eruption from your inner depth that fundamentally alters the outer landscape of your life.

VULNERABILITY & CHANGE

Genuine change, and the vulnerability that accompanies it, often emerges when an unexpected circumstance or crisis occurs in our life. This crisis opens us to the newest edges of our life journey. All seasons of living, joyful or painful, have a rich purpose. Typically, we resist changes that carry any element of pain or suffering. For example, facing a possible divorce or job loss. We are often inclined to think that it is not OK for changes to happen and thus fight against them, rather than recognize the gifts and the learnings that are unfolding right in front of us. Life's painful experiences are not designed to make us suffer, but to crack us open. We may suffer, yes, but that is not their purpose.

One of the ways the Divine flows through us is through an array of human emotions that are ever-revealing themselves. Emotions are intimately involved in change, yet they are not always pretty or comfortable. A key to navigating your emotions is developing the ability to fully experience them while not being taken over by them. Being vulnerable means allowing yourself to feel uncomfortable in unfamiliar territory.

One of the more powerful illustrations of transformative change in the natural world involves the caterpillar. At a certain point in its existence, it is compelled by instinct to construct a cocoon around itself so it can enter a passage of metamorphosis that will result in emerging from the cocoon as a butterfly. Astonishingly, there is a middle stage in this transformative process in which, inside the cocoon, it is neither a caterpillar nor a butterfly—it is an almost entirely fluid substance!

Interestingly, scientists have discovered that there is inherent resistance within the body of the caterpillar to this process of transformation. There are clumps of cells called "imaginal cells," which are contained within the caterpillar's body throughout its life and are the essential elements of the butterfly-to-be. During metamorphosis, these imaginal cells suddenly begin to divide more and more rapidly. At first, these cells are treated as invaders and attacked by the caterpillar's immune system. But eventually the number of imaginal cells overwhelm the dwindling caterpillar cells and begin to use the raw materials around them to assemble new butterfly structures, such as wings, legs, eyes and antennae. At the completion of this process, a whole butterfly is formed and begins emerging from the cocoon.

Many of us can relate to this unsettling yet essential experience, one of disintegration and then reintegration. During times of vulnerability, we seek protection by holding on to the image of ourselves as we have been. A lot of breaking into freedom is about recognizing what aspects of your life no longer carry vitality—and which new aspects are emerging!

Life is comprised of beginnings, middles and endings. Given the vulnerability that accompanies beginnings and endings, most of us have a tendency to try and expand the middles as long as possible to avoid discomfort and change. By doing so, we often increase our pain and deny ourselves rich growth possibilities.

The key here is that all meaningful change asks you to genuinely surrender to something that is largely unknown. Eventually, you come to the frontier of your life and are asked to face both the difficulties and blessings that are unfolding. Courage, transparency and steady support are required to step forward onto the uncharted paths that become the new ground of your life.

Invitation for Discovery

1. I invite you to reflect upon your path of evolution and identify a time of radical change that swept through your life, when a whole new and unexpected season of expression arrived on the scene. In your *Journal*, capture any vivid memories from this rich experience.

2. Take a moment to survey the different dimensions of your current life. What one area in particular might be most fertile for groundbreaking transformation? Note as well any emotions you may experience as you bring new eyes and imagination towards these areas.

COURAGEOUS CONVERSATIONS

Embracing change involves entering into courageous conversations with emerging aspects inside yourself—as well as the people that truly matter in your life.

Inwardly, deeper parts of yourself—those with knowing and desire—are talking to you, attempting to get your attention so you will heed their requests. Outwardly, when change is upon you, you are often asked to have a more direct and truthful conversation with others. It can be frightening to risk being courageously transparent. Courageous conversations are vulnerable because they involve entering the unknown, and invariably are the ones you don't want to have.

To step past your false self and its fears, some measure of inner wrestling is a natural part of the change process. No step is too small. In truth, while making that next phone call or scheduling that next business meeting may make you vulnerable and require bravery, it also has the potential to radically change the course of your outer life.

Invitation for Discovery

I invite you to take identify in your *Journal* one courageous conversation that you know needs to take place with someone in your life. Perhaps it is one that you have been avoiding for some time, and your intuition is becoming more insistent that you risk moving forward. If you sense the timing is ripe for action, even if you may be fearful, I invite you to commit to having this conversation with them. I encourage you to prepare for your conversation by calming your nerves, and by bringing forward a sincere openness to an unexpected outcome.

SACRED PASSAGES

Our lives are comprised of a steady flow of what I call sacred passages. We are always traversing sacred passages of some kind, and often more than one at any given time. It could be the experience of going through college, or the process of courting our first love. Another would be the process of getting engaged and married. Pregnancy and bringing a new Soul into the world is another sacred passage, as is starting a new career or buying a new home. Dealing with significant loss is yet another sacred passage.

A sacred passage compels you to bring your focused attention towards some aspect of your life that is unfolding in a powerful new way. It's a sustained period of engagement in which you have an opportunity to learn new things about yourself, a gateway that may likely be as transformative as it is disruptive.

Everything that has happened to me—navigating my brother's and sister's challenges, my dad's cancer and the ways it transformed us both, my healing relationship with Zena, my involvement with USM, my awakening relationship with Spirit—were all sacred passages that have made up my hero's journey.

When you identify and honor the sacred passages that are currently taking place in your life, your Authentic Self is supported in thriving. All humans go through seasons of fear, loss and contraction—as well as expansion and transformation. Conscious acknowledgement of a sacred passage, including a painful one, supports you in fully harvesting its particular learnings and gifts.

It's critical to be aware of the kinds of support you might need to fully embrace a sacred passage. When you follow the path of vulnerability, you come face-to-face with the necessity of asking for help. In our modern culture, we have a tendency to place a high premium upon being independent, while often not recognizing the leveraging power of healthy interdependence. Having assistance can make all the difference in the ease with which you traverse a sacred passage, as well as in maximizing the harvest of learnings you receive from it.

Human beings have a tendency, when we can't see how to get from point A to point B, to think that somehow we are inadequate. Actually, we have arrived in the gifted territory of realizing how important it is to ask for assistance from visible and invisible sources. Doing so with vulnerable honesty can move mountains.

It can be quite empowering to coin a creative name or phrase for the current sacred passage you are traversing in your life. For instance, Season of Determination, Healing Loss, or Well-Earned Triumph. Rich, descriptive titles can be clarifying and help you to consciously remember that the passage you are traversing is an essential chapter in your hero's journey. Using your creative imagination to frame your life experience in this way connects you more deeply with the unique opportunities being gifted to you as you traverse this sacred passage.

Attuning to the underlying essence of life serves life, and each sacred passage you go through is an opportunity to strengthen your connection with your Authentic Self.

Invitation for Discovery

1. a) I invite you to identify a sacred passage you've recently completed in your life.
   b) As we often forget to truly acknowledge and savor ourselves, our experiences, and our life's unfoldment, reflect upon the gifts and learnings this sacred passage gave you.
   c) See if a name or phrase or a symbol for this completed season of your life is revealed to you (for example: Spreading My Wings, or Courageous Flowering, etc.).
   d) Write a note of gratitude to Spirit or your Authentic Self for the gifts that flowed your way during this passage.

2. a) Now, identify a sacred passage you're currently going through (or may soon begin).
   b) What gifts and learnings might this sacred passage hold for you?
   c) See if a name or phrase or a symbol for this next season of your life is revealed to you.
   d) What assistance might you need to traverse this passage successfully?
   e) What would be your very next step to secure the support needed?
   f) Record your responses in your *Journal*.

LIFE IS A DARING ADVENTURE

by Helen Keller

Security is mostly a superstition.
It does not exist in nature,
nor do the children of men as a whole experience it.
Avoiding danger is no safer in the long run
than outright exposure.
Life is a daring adventure,
or nothing.
To keep our faces toward change
and behave like free spirits
in the presence of fate is strength
and undefeatable.

IN SWEET COMPANY

by Margaret Wolff

We sit together and I tell you things,
Silent, unborn, naked things
That only my God has heard me say.
You do not cluck your tongue at me
Or roll your eyes
Or split my heart into a thousand pieces
With words that have little to do with me.
You do not turn away because you cannot bear to see
Your own unclaimed light shining in my eyes.
You stay with me in the dark.
You urge me into being.
You make room in your heart for my voice.
You rejoice in my joy.
And through it all, you stand unbound
By everything but the still, small Voice within you.
I see my future Self in you
Just enough to risk
Moving beyond the familiar,
Just enough to leave
The familiar in the past where it belongs.
I breathe you in and breathe you out
In one luxurious and contented sigh.
In sweet company
I am home at last.

CHAPTER 8

Intimate Relationship: The Ultimate Mirror

"A relationship that you give yourself over to is a powerful apprenticeship to the person you are continually evolving to be."

~ David Whyte

SHARING WHAT IS MOST ALIVE IN US

Authentic relationship involves sharing what is most alive in us with our partner. This may be joy, sadness, surprise, disappointment, grief—whatever we may be experiencing at any given moment. To become and remain open to a steady flow of generous intimacy with one another, each partner must be dedicated to cultivating a rich connection with their inner life, which then becomes available to pour into the outer relationship.

A committed intimate relationship has 2 primary purposes. One is the extraordinary joy of companionship, of being able to share life's journey together. The second purpose is to support each partner in healing their unresolved issues and evolving to their fullest potential.

Thus, making a commitment to a partner can be a powerful vehicle for becoming more aware and deepening the connection with our Authentic Self. If consciously and skillfully approached, a loving partnership provides us with a fierce and tender laboratory for self-discovery.

EVOLVING BEYOND ROMANTIC IDEALISM

Through the influence of fairy tales, movies, songs and the pervading media culture that surrounded us growing up, most of us have developed a perfectionist ideal of romantic love that is distorted and unsustainable.

We understandably become enamored when an attractive new person initially enters our life. We have a tendency to magnify in our mind those qualities that enrapture us, and craft our image and expectations of our partner almost exclusively around these traits. In the early stages of relationship, often flowing from sexual chemistry and a shared emotional resonance, we often make the mistake of believing that we know our partner better than we really do. In truth, we don't yet know this person deeply or well.

As humans, we often unconsciously look to our partner to make us more whole. They can't, however, since nothing outside of us can truly complete us. These unreasonable expectations undermine the cultivation of true intimacy and long-term success in a love relationship.

To dispel another myth, true love does not equal love without conflict. Not even the healthiest relationships escape the inevitable days and subtle patterns of pain, frustration, disappointment and loneliness, and even the occasional desire to bolt. Even though love often starts as a dream come true, there are times when it may feel like it is devolving into our worst nightmare. With the exception of an abusive relationship, which is essential to discern, these experiences are a natural part of a healthy, evolving relationship.

We all have traumas from unmet childhood needs, and are a little bit crazy in our own unique ways. To move beyond the unreasonable expectation that a relationship should always travel in smooth waters, it is far healthier to appreciate that both partners are flawed and sometimes challenging to live with. In light of this, humility is a cornerstone of healthy intimacy.

The initial stage of a relationship is not the high point, it is just the opening act of what has the potential to be a more enduring and fulfilling journey. Most of us certainly feel "high on love" in an extraordinary way in the beginning, yet this emotional heat tends to cool off over time once greater familiarity is established. For those who move through life always looking for the next "high," the process of sobering up in a relationship can feel like a loss. This can then lead to further loss if one or both partners go off in search of the next "high." The healthy alternative is riding the waves, allowing the fantasy dimension to fade, and allowing a more grounded, satisfying reality to evolve in its place—one that is based on shared interests, values and loving affection.

Love, in this context, is not a state of unwavering enthusiasm, it's an actual day-to-day spiritual practice. The healthy process of investing and deepening in a long-term relationship requires dedicated inner work, and often centers more upon us growing up within ourselves than upon pinpointing what is right or wrong about our partner.

A committed, loving partnership is an astonishing attempt by two remarkable yet flawed human creatures to do the best they can to meet each other's needs while also fulfilling their own. In this process, the core qualities that support couples as they learn about and adapt to each other are safety, patience and tenderness. Establishing this generous, compassionate orientation to intimacy significantly increases the likelihood that both partners will invest in the inner work required for their love to flourish and endure.

Invitation for Discovery

1. I invite you to capture in your *Journal* one specific belief you hold, based on a romantic ideal, about how intimate relationships "should" be. How might you shift this view to be more realistic and compassionate? Note any sense of relief and release that might come with this changed perspective.

2. I invite you to reflect upon a specific partner, past or present, from your life with whom you entered into a committed relationship. How did you feel about this person in the beginning? What developed between you and how did it turn out? From a perspective of compassionate learning, how might you have

handled problematic situations differently to produce a healthier dynamic? Do you see any opportunities to put your learning into practice in your current relationships?

3. Take some time to capture your reflections and insights in your *Journal*.

WELCOMING INTIMACY INTO MY LIFE

After joining the University of Santa Monica faculty and successfully establishing my private practice, I wrote out what I called a living vision of the woman I desired to welcome into my life as my wife, long-term life partner and future mother of our children. I was 30 years old.

Two years later, I met my beloved while facilitating a USM retreat in 1987. She was a student completing the final course of her Master's degree in Spiritual Psychology.

On the first evening of the retreat, Susan stood up and shared within the large class. As soon as my eyes met hers, my heart was deeply stirred. It seemed I may have finally connected with the woman I'd prayed for, someone who carried the qualities I'd been steadily envisioning for years. She later shared with me that at the moment she first saw me, she inwardly heard the words, "There is the man I'd like to be the father of my son."

We started dating from across the country, as I lived in Southern California and Susan and her 6-year-old daughter, Alaya, lived in Philadelphia. To bridge the distance between us, we would record extended musings and reflections with each other on audio cassettes and send them back and forth across the country (this was before there was an internet!). We were determined to reveal ourselves to each other as honestly as possible, and the process of regularly recording without pauses or editing took courage and commitment. We continually risked sharing more deeply with each other, even as we feared the possibility of being rejected. I can remember many times when, the moment after dropping the envelope with my newly recorded cassette into the blue postbox on my street corner, I wanted to climb into the box to grab it because I was afraid of what I had just dared to reveal to Susan. I still have all those cassettes she sent me as part of my sacred library.

After a few months, Susan flew out to Los Angeles to spend a week together. When I saw her at the airport, I was astonished to find myself immediately challenged by how much shorter she was than I had remembered. I felt terrible that I hadn't recognized her height as a serious issue when I met her at the retreat. I think I was blinded by the strength of our spiritual connection.

Susan is 5'2" and I am 6'3'. At that moment, my inner dialogue went along the lines of, "The woman I am to marry is supposed to be tall. This isn't right." I was remembering Zena, my first girlfriend, who was almost 6-feet tall, which I'm sure highly influenced my imaginings. Thus, my romanticized picture of my future partner had included my prayerful request that she be tall.

I was confronted with a challenging and embarrassing predicament. The genuine question I faced was whether I wanted to continue dating Susan at all. Yet, here she was at the airport, having flown across the country to be together. The next question I faced soon revealed itself: "Was I brave enough to tell her the truth about my thoughts and how I felt?"

I judged myself as being extremely superficial for holding this preference. I wondered if I should even talk to Susan about it because she clearly couldn't change how tall she was. Yet, to some very insistent aspect within me, the height of my partner was extremely important. And Susan literally didn't appear to be measuring up!

Knowing an authentic relationship was essential to me, I decided to be transparent and risk sharing everything. I was prepared for her to be reactive and to judge me. When I shared my truth with her, she was, of course, visibly shaken and upset. She did not react towards me, however, nor make me wrong or judge me. She actually acknowledged me for being brave enough to tell her my truth. It was a very raw passage, as we both knew this was the kind of issue that might halt our courtship in its tracks.

When we arrived at my apartment, she gently asked if I would be willing to sit and hold a safe space for her while she did some inner work. I said sure. She laid down on the carpeted floor on her back with her knees up, her hands on her belly, and she started to cry. She wept deeply. Susan communicated out loud to an aspect inside of her she called her Little One that it was safe to feel and share, and that she was there in support and love. Her Little One expressed that she really liked me, and was fearful I would reject her. This place inside of her was sad that our relationship might end before it had really begun, and also felt helpless. As Susan worked with her Little One, she tenderly kept her hands on her belly as she invited herself to feel all of her emotions. From time to time, between her tears, she said to her Little One, "It's okay, Sweetheart. It's okay to feel all of that. I'm here for you and it's safe. I want to know what you're experiencing, please keep sharing."

Susan's healing and tender work with herself took about 20 minutes. At the completion of their sharing, she said to her Little One, "Look, I don't know what he is going to do or if he wants to be with us. But I want you to know that no matter what he chooses, I will be here with you. I will never leave you, and I will always love you just the way you are."

I was deeply moved by this healing exchange. My heart was stirred by how she entered into such a profound space of love with and for herself. I respected how she took 100% responsibility for her own emotions that were triggered by my sharing. I also admired how she facilitated the inner dialogue with her Little One, a practice that she had learned in the USM program. A profound reservoir of love for Susan awakened in me.

This experience did not derail our courtship—it deepened it. Amazingly, my issue with Susan's height disappeared as she was completing her inner work on the floor of my apartment. Her height became irrelevant to me. From that point forward, she seemed tall in my eyes.

Who Susan was, and what she did that day, strengthened our sacred connection with each other. It also blessed us in another way: it served to establish a precedent for how we would hold a safe space for each other whenever either of us had an opportunity to work with our emotional disturbances in a healing way.

EMOTIONAL TRIGGERS: OUR GATEWAY TO HEALING & GROWTH

All trauma, and all healing from trauma, takes place through the rich vessel of our relationships with others. A committed intimate relationship offers us the greatest opportunity to unwind our wounds. Harville Hendrix's well-known Imago Therapy for couples builds on the premise that individuals are unconsciously attracted to partners who encompass their caregivers' positive and negative traits in an attempt to resolve unmet childhood needs.

Having a safe space with someone we deeply care about can provide us with potent opportunities to expose and face our human frailties in a conscious and creative way. One of the ways that this occurs is when our unconscious thoughts and feelings bubble to the surface, triggered unexpectedly during the course of our daily interactions with our partner. When this happens, it can seem like an unfortunate and highly embarrassing misstep has occurred.

What most couples do not recognize is that a committed, loving partnership is actually functioning optimally when it triggers unresolved issues within each partner. While this process is not easy or comfortable, a relationship is the perfect container for each partner to become conscious of and process painful emotional debris from their past. These experiences can support us in recognizing the life-altering and lingering misinterpretations of reality we formed early in our life in response to confusing and hurtful experiences.

For instance, a woman who was emotionally and verbally abused by her father during childhood may have mistakenly concluded that all men are cruel and dangerous. Later in life, when her partner expresses any measure of anger, she may feel a terror that is out of all proportion to the present situation. As she becomes aware of this unconscious "programming," she has the opportunity to update her beliefs to reflect a healed and more mature perspective about herself, her partner, and life in general. She might begin to understand and trust, for example, that anger—when expressed safely and constructively—is a natural and healthy emotion.

When we do get emotionally triggered in relationship, the central block to healthy intimacy is projection—a misinterpretation of our partner's behavior based upon our faulty, trauma-based assumptions. We all have unconscious issues, and when we get triggered, our initial tendency is often to blame our partner for what we're feeling and to make them wrong. In essence, we mistakenly assume that the cause of our disturbance is their behavior. In actuality, the disturbance is one we have been carrying in our unconscious long before our partner ever came into our life. This is not meant to imply that there are no abusive partners, it's more about learning how to optimally use a healthy partnership in service to each other's highest evolution.

When our inner peace is disrupted while we are engaged in intimate relationship, often the wisest course of action is to acknowledge this awareness to your partner and, if needed, gently step away from interacting with them for a period of time. By wisely stepping back from interacting with our partner when we are triggered, we avoid emotional escalation and can turn our full attention to the place inside of us that is upset.

If we are dedicated to inner growth, we need to learn to tolerate and embrace our vulnerable edges when they inevitably make their appearance. We can give these emotions a voice and learn about their disturbance and what they might need from us. This is what Susan did on the floor of my apartment when she was afraid I might reject her because she wasn't as tall as I thought my partner should be.

By not reacting to or blaming our partner, we disengage from the mistaken assumption that our disturbance is primarily an issue about the outer relationship. Not blaming our partner for our upset makes us available to new levels of truth and healing in our inner world. Invariably, as we consciously explore the emotional pain that has been triggered, we often discover unresolved trauma we've been carrying from our past. These places inside that are making themselves known to us often simply need our recognition, understanding and compassion.

If each partner is willing to approach emotional disturbances in the relationship in this way, they can harvest one of the richest gifts available through intimate partnership—that of supporting and witnessing each other's healing journey.

SURRENDERING TO LOVE

From the very first time I experienced her radiant presence and joyful voice, I was asked to surrender to the strength of Susan's softness and loving. During the initial season of our courtship, I often found myself frightened by the amount of love she poured my way. While my parents were loving, my home was often in chaos, and I simply didn't grow up with this level of unconditional love. It was scary for me to continue opening my heart to her. The core false self pattern that was triggered by Susan's love was my fear of being abandoned. In essence, deep down, I was afraid that if Susan really got to know me, she would leave me.

I sometimes felt out of control, and unconsciously kept trying to run away from our intimacy. In fact, a little over a year after we were together, I somehow convinced myself that we needed to break off our relationship, and so I did.

Right after I broke up with Susan—and, amazingly, she just kept loving me when I did—I boarded a plane to fly from Philadelphia to Los Angeles. After take off, I began listening to some of Susan's music with her angelic, healing voice. With my eyes closed, I connected with an anxious little boy inside of me. He was terrified. He told me that he was afraid that if I committed myself to Susan, she would eventually be dissatisfied and leave me. I then realized that I was attempting to protect myself by leaving her before she left me.

Despite the fact that I was sitting in the middle seat, with passengers on my left and right, the little boy inside of me suddenly began sobbing loudly and uncontrollably. As I was crying, I heard the following words being spoken to me from a deep place in my heart: "You have no right to walk away from what we have given you. This relationship is more than you could ever imagine—you have no right."

At that moment, all the fears or doubts I had been carrying about being with Susan dissolved. I suddenly knew without question that I was a worthy man and partner, and that I no longer needed to protect myself. I don't know whether this was a voice from God or my higher Self. It didn't matter. All I knew at the time is that these words were undeniably true. It was clear that invisible forces were supporting me to continue opening my heart to Susan.

As I gave myself permission to feel these deep emotions fully, I felt physically relieved to be released from the grip of fear and unworthiness that had had a hold of me since my dark teen years. When my flight landed and I got back to my apartment, I called Susan and relayed to her the inner directive I'd received. With great tenderness, she conveyed to me she understood. Soon after this experience, she moved to Los Angeles with her daughter and we began building our lives together. Shortly afterwards, I proposed to her and we got married.

THE WISDOM OF TIMEOUTS

Almost 80% of harmful discord in intimate relationships—including saying things we regret, being frustrated, expressing anger, and judging our partner—can be eliminated by simply taking a timeout when our interactions with each other first begin to escalate and get heated. To avoid destructive blowups, each partner has to be willing to take responsibility for their behavior when things turn tense and reactive. It is wise to call a timeout and disengage from interacting with each other in order to provide the space needed to restore our emotional balance.

When we are emotionally triggered and upset, we have a hard time staying connected with our own love. Our connection with our partner can also be eclipsed by the depth of our triggered emotions from the past, which is often disproportionate to the situation at hand. As well, our mind often conjures up a story to justify our reason for being upset. When we are in this reactive state, we are best served by not totally buying into or acting out based on our thoughts, and by beginning to simply witness them.

If either partner feels an escalation of tension in the relationship in a charged moment, they can simply say, "I am starting to get triggered here. I'm starting to get upset. I'd like to disengage and take some time with my own process." This is not a power maneuver or avoidance strategy, nor is it an intention to punish your partner. If the request is spoken with sincerity, and a mutual understanding exists that there will be a circling back with each other once the tides are calm, a timeout simply says, "I recognize the space between us is getting agitated. I care about us, so let's reconnect later and talk about this when we're both calmer."

Once both partners are willing to see a timeout as a sacred and mutually beneficial act, it becomes an offering, a way of honoring each other. It's about taking care of and stewarding the relationship. As partners more consistently disengage whenever needed, greater levels of safety flow into the partnership. The ability to find honorable ground to stand upon during challenges—while staying connected with each other—can be steadily strengthened and trusted.

MY ACHILLES HEEL

Throughout our courtship and subsequent marriage, Susan and I continued supporting each other in working with our emotional disturbances whenever they surfaced. Due to the depth of trauma I experienced in my family, starting when I was 10 years old, my pattern of angry outbursts whenever I became physically frustrated continued to be a challenge. They occurred every couple of months and this was hard on our relationship.

It was an Easter morning in the early 90's. I was trying to print some last minute materials I needed for a workshop and the printer wasn't cooperating. I could feel my frustration rapidly mounting, and I found myself yelling, "Are you fucking kidding me? Why the hell won't you work?" This clearly wasn't helping the printing process, but I felt trapped and out of control. After several minutes of disturbing the whole household with angry words, I finally found my breath. I gave myself a timeout and took a long walk.

I checked in with my emotions, inquiring what this anger was all about. I gave myself time to feel and express my upset. Settling into this process as I walked, now more calm, I explored what was hiding beneath the depth of rage. As I did, I came to a realization that underneath my anger, I had for decades unwittingly stored up feelings of grief and helplessness from my traumatic teenage years. I allowed myself to feel more vulnerable, and met my hurt feelings with tenderness and compassion.

After I completed my inner healing process, I reconnected with Susan and shared these realizations. I remember standing together in the garage as I told her what I had learned, and sincerely apologizing to her for my cross words. She was immensely grateful that I was able to touch into the hurt underneath my anger. It was a watershed turn in our marriage, as from that time forward I was more able to bypass my angry outbursts and bring healing to my hurt feelings whenever they surfaced. My ability to be patient with myself whenever I began getting frustrated steadily increased. After many years of wrestling with this painful pattern, I was making substantial progress in my emotional maturity. I was so grateful that we had cultivated a safe space in our partnership to bring forward this healing.

FACILITATING OUR INNER WORK

As painful as they are, disturbances that take place in our close relationships are pure gold offered for us to harvest. Intimacy empowers us to consciously recognize that which we have yet to see—in essence, to become unblind. In service to ourselves and our partner, it is wise to take maximum advantage of these opportunities to move deeper in our relationship with ourselves. We've earned the right to responsibly heal and become more whole.

We take timeouts from interacting with our partner to bring ourselves back into emotional balance and, most importantly, to engage in a process of reflection and learning. During a timeout, each partner can employ a range of supportive awareness tools to discover what's really taking place under the surface of their own emotional reactivity. Taking a reflective walk in nature, as well as journaling, are two such tools which can support us in coming back into balance. As well, some find the leverage of professional therapeutic support invaluable in their transformational process. The process of discovering old wounds and traumas, in a setting of empathy and safety, is a golden opportunity to meet our unmet needs from the past.

Susan's inner work on the floor of my apartment is an example of the kind of compassionate connection that can be established with ourself—and how effective it can be for dealing with our upset when we are triggered. After a needed timeout to come into greater balance within ourselves, we are more prepared to reconnect with our partner in an honorable way following times of misunderstanding and disharmony.

"Sometimes the truth depends upon a good walk around the lake."
~ William Carlos Williams

Invitation for Discovery

1. I invite you to reflect upon a time when you were emotionally triggered during a confrontation with an intimate partner. What were some of your specific behaviors that played out as your upset escalated?

2. As you revisit this encounter, what can you see more clearly and learn about yourself?

3. I encourage you to set an intention to employ constructive, Self-supportive strategies the next time you are upset with someone you care about. In addition to wisely taking a timeout, what other ways might you gently and effectively support yourself?

RECONNECTING IN SAFETY & CURIOSITY

To be in a committed relationship where we feel truly listened to and understood by our partner is a rare and precious experience in life. We all long to feel seen, heard, understood, accepted and loved. We reserve our most intimate thoughts and feelings for the people who provide an open space where we feel safe to express and be received without judgment.

There is one crucial variable which determines the degree to which a committed intimate relationship is actually flourishing: if each partner is sincerely committed to understanding and cherishing their partner's experience as much as they understand and cherish their own experience. To truly care about and inquire of our partner's nuanced experience of their life journey—totally independent of whether it matches our experience, and whether or not we agree with it—is a sacred offering.

WHEN SOMEONE DEEPLY LISTENS TO YOU

by John Fox

When someone deeply listens to you
it is like holding out a dented cup
you've had since childhood
and watching it fill up with
cold, fresh water.
When it balances on top of the brim,
you are understood.
When it overflows and touches your skin,
you are loved.

When someone deeply listens to you,
the room where you stay
starts a new life
and the place where you wrote
your first poem
begins to glow in your mind's eye.
It is as if gold has been discovered!

When someone deeply listens to you,
your bare feet are on the earth
and a beloved land that seemed distant
is now at home within you.

Invitation for Discovery

I invite you to select a person you are in a close relationship with who would be willing to participate in an exercise of heartfelt listening. Sit across from each other, and take turns openly sharing whatever is present for 5 minutes each. The listener is afforded the freedom of simply listening without interpreting, interrupting, asking questions, or verbally intervening in any way. At the completion of each round, the listener can simply say, "Thank you for sharing." Continue to rotate turns until you both feel complete. This process can open each partner to the healing that comes when our inner experience is simply heard and understood. Capture in your *Journal* any revelations from this exercise, both from your experience as a sharer and as a listener.

THE POWER OF APOLOGY

Stephen and Ondrea Levine's book, Embracing the Beloved, beautifully captures the tender territory of relationship and how it can serve as an awakening ground for each partner's evolution in consciousness. They speak about continually bringing mercy, or forgiveness, towards our partner. As compassion is at the heart of forgiveness, a sincere apology can be a sacred act in its potential to reopen our hearts.

Apologizing used to feel like a defeat to me. I would feel embarrassed and humiliated whenever I would apologize. Susan patiently taught me that whenever I recognized I'd been emotionally reactive towards her, I could honestly and proactively come to her and say something like, "I want to confess something. I realize in that last conversation, I was trying to be right. I was trying to score points, and I was irritated towards you. I see that now and I'm sincerely sorry. I want to do my best not to do this again." With practice, the honorable action of a heartfelt apology felt more and more natural for me.

In a healthy relationship, both partners can acknowledge their errors and learnings, and sincerely apologize to each other in a heartfelt way. This amplifies the safety in the relationship, because when honesty and humility reign, our false self's protective mechanisms don't have a chance to get a foothold.

THE BLESSINGS OF AUTHENTIC RELATIONSHIP

In a long-term committed relationship, we live on an evolving frontier. As each partner becomes more anchored in their Authentic Self, there will always be new risks, new levels of healing, and new ways to dance together. This is because we will feel continually safer to allow deeper levels of our previously hidden selves to emerge—to be witnessed, forgiven, and transformed. We will always be discovering rough edges which can be softened, as healing is a lifelong process.

When a committed relationship actively supports each partner's emotional maturation, more and more of the couple's energy is available to simply enjoy each other. A flourishing partnership also serves as a vital wellspring of support which empowers each partner in successfully manifesting their individual dreams and gifted expressions. These are the blessings afforded when each partner is willing to wholeheartedly embrace their inner work.

THE KNOWING

by Sharon Olds

Afterwards, when we have slept, paradise-
comaed, and woken, we lie a long time
looking at each other. I do not know what
he sees, but I see eyes of unsurpassing tenderness
and calm, a calm like the dignity of matter.

I love the open ocean
blue-grey-green of his iris, I love
the curve of it against the white,
that curve the sight of what has caused me
to come, when he's quite still, deep
inside me. I have never seen a curve
like that, except the earth from outer

space.

I don't know where he got
his kindness without self-regard,
almost without self, and yet
he chose one woman, instead of the others.
By knowing him, I get to know
the purity of the animal
which mates for life.

Sometimes he is slightly
smiling, but mostly he just gazes at me gazing,
his entire face lit. I love to see it change if I cry
—there is no worry, no pity, a graver radiance.

If we are on our backs, side by side,
with our faces turned fully to face each other,
I can hear a tear from my lower eye
hit the sheet, as if it is an early day on earth,
and then the upper eye's tears
braid and sluice down through the lower eyebrow
like the invention of farming, irrigation, a non-nomadic people.
I am so lucky that I know him.
This is the only way to know him.
I am the only one who knows him.

When I wake again, he is still looking at me,
as if he is eternal. For an hour
we wake and doze, and slowly I know

that though we are sated, though we are hardly
touching, this is the coming the other
coming brought us to the edge of — we are entering,
deeper and deeper, gaze by gaze,
this place beyond the other places,
beyond the body itself,
we are making love.

THE GUEST HOUSE

by Jelaluddin Rumi

This being human is a guest house.
Every morning a new arrival

A joy, a depression, a meanness,
Some momentary awareness comes
As an unexpected visitor

Welcome and entertain them all!
Even if they're a crowd of sorrows,
Who violently sweep your house
Empty of its furniture

Still, treat each guest honorably.
He may be clearing you out
For some new delight.

The dark thought, shame, the malice,
Meet them at the door laughing,
And invite them in.

Be grateful for whoever comes,
Because each has been sent
As a guest from beyond.

CHAPTER 9

Multiplicity of Selves: Healing Our Inner Family

"It takes courage to enter your inner world and bring to the surface what you find."

~ Roderick W. MacIver

EMBRACING MULTIPLICITY

In our culture, most of us make the mistaken assumption that at any given moment we only have a singular identity. The term multiplicity of selves refers not only to our ever-changing thoughts and feelings, as described in Rumi's poem, *The Guest House*, it also points to the diverse dimensions that make up the totality of who we are. Among these dimensions are the physical, emotional, mental, sexual, imaginative and spiritual levels of our experience.

By now you are familiar with two dynamic aspects that live within each of us: the Authentic Self and the false self, also referred to as the adapted self. Each of these has its unique approach to and experience of reality. In this chapter, you will also be introduced to other key selves that reside in our inner world, including our Inner Child. Later in the book, in Section Three, we'll be discussing the feminine and masculine energies within our consciousness.

The Authentic Self is capable of facilitating compassionate leadership in your consciousness. It acts from sovereignty and is an all-embracing, neutral witness to the multitude of aspects that reside within it. As you grow accustomed to consciously living from this center, you continually learn how to honor and give voice to all your inner selves and experiences. Healthy multiplicity flows from this co-existing community of selves.

We tend to identify with our current thoughts and feelings and believe that they singularly define who we are. Thus we say, "I am depressed," or, "I am angry." As an example of multiplicity, it would be more accurate to say, "A part of me is depressed," or, "I feel angry." By relating to your experience in this way, you are not completely identifying your whole self with whatever you are feeling at any given moment. Your feelings of depression or anger are only one aspect of your inner experience. Recognizing this distinction, especially during those times when what you are feeling is intensely experienced in the body, allows you to make room for, accept and cooperate with the flow of deep emotions moving through you.

Having contradictory feelings is commonplace. The greater the emotional stakes you have invested in any relationship or set of circumstances, the more likely you are to experience a range of feelings. This is partly why the neutrality of the Authentic Self is so healing and comforting, as it resides beyond polarization and the distress that often accompanies internal contradictions.

Consider the experience of moving out of state for a job promotion. On the one hand, you feel the grief of leaving your current job and your rooted relationships with close friends and family. At the same time, you are enthused by the possibility of new adventures and the leadership opportunities that await you in your new job. Both feelings are completely natural for you to experience in this situation, and both can be compassionately acknowledged and embraced.

OUR AUTHENTIC SELF AS UNIFYING CENTER

Most of us, if we are fortunate, are able to reflect upon precious times we have spent with a truly close friend or loved one—someone who knew us well, accepted us fully, and with whom we felt free to express ourselves without fear of being judged. It is essential for us to recognize that a healing and expansive relationship of this caliber can also be cultivated and become available to us *inwardly*—in our relationship with our Authentic Self.

As you build a conscious relationship with this wellspring of your true nature, you cultivate greater safety and spaciousness. You are then able to move on from being stuck or over-identified with any particular feeling, thought, or behavior that you have. In this way, you can achieve greater balance among these various aspects without being constrained by any of them. This is empowering. Your Authentic Self serves as the unifying center of your inner world, always present as a source of support and guidance.

AN INNER PARTNERSHIP

I was waiting to be introduced and go on stage to give a talk in front of several hundred people. The subject of my talk was Embracing Vulnerability. I was aware at that moment of a part of me that was feeling anxious and insecure. This inner aspect had thoughts like, "Who do I think I am? Do I <u>really</u> have anything worthwhile to say?" followed immediately by an answer, "I don't think so." This part of me was scared. I scanned the room for an exit and began considering how I might justify a last-minute departure.

I took a deep breath and turned my attention inwardly to investigate my experience further. My Authentic Self, who was observing, was all too aware of this anxious place. This wasn't the first time this had occurred for me. Quite the contrary. I was very familiar with this fearful voice. It was the presence of unworthiness that arose whenever I was afraid of being judged by others. I recognized I was identifying with the voice of my false self.

My True Self listened to this aspect with tender compassion and talked to it in a reassuring way, letting it know that we were capable of giving an excellent talk. I gently placed my hand on my belly, the part of my body where I felt my anxiety. Inwardly, I said to this place, "I know you are scared, but we will be fine, and I will hold your hand as we walk through this experience together."

A few minutes later, once I was introduced and began the talk, a flow of wisdom and quiet confidence moved through me. The Teacher aspect within, which I also carry, arrived front and center, which was a common experience for me. I openly shared with the group the vulnerable process that had just taken place prior to stepping on stage. I relayed to them how I supported myself through my experience of insecurity, and about how we are all multi-dimensional in nature, and that we are all susceptible to feelings of inadequacy and imperfection. Throughout my talk, this less courageous aspect of me rested inside, thankful that it had been able to express its fears and be heard, and grateful to be embraced by the strength and compassion of my Authentic Self.

OUR MIND

The mind is a powerful tool that serves us in many ways. Among other things, it tracks and categorizes information, and can assist us in holding a clear focus as we participate in and take action in the world. It has significant limitations, however, when we over-identify with it and mistake its thoughts as representative of our deeper nature. When we give our power away to the mind, it acts like a regent that has usurped the power of the throne from the rightful ruler of our life—our Authentic Self. Thus, while the mind can be a great servant when we learn how to use it effectively, it is not a trustworthy leader.

The ego, which for many is synonymous with the false self, is the aspect of the mind that often endeavors to protect and control us like a dominating parent. It is both directive and reactive in an attempt to control our environment. It is often dominated by fear, defensiveness, and, at times, an obsession to fulfill our unmet needs in unhealthy ways. In essence, addictive behaviors are an expression of our false self and our body looking for love in all the wrong places.

One of the other limitations of the mind is its tendency to assert itself as our ultimate authority. It often makes a presumption of knowing, and does so by concluding that things are either good or bad, right or wrong. If left to its own devices, it invariably enters into negative judgment. This orientation only breeds an experience of internal separation and disharmony.

Thankfully, your True Self does not reside in your mind's field of judgment and is the calm witness to any conflicts that arise in your inner world. Without its guiding presence, your various subpersonalities will continue to drive your psychological car, each demanding its turn at the wheel. As you establish a more conscious relationship with your Authentic Self, the limiting aspects of your critical mind dissolve and soften over time because you are no longer giving them your attention and power.

"Out beyond ideas of wrong-doing and right-doing, there is a field. I'll meet you there."

~ Rumi

EPIPHANY

It was 1987 and I was co-facilitating a USM class in Philadelphia. As I walked up to the stage, I once again felt a rising anxiety. I became aware of a judgment I was holding against myself as an incompetent teacher. At that moment, an epiphany permeated my core: "Judgment is an absolute waste of time." The wise part of me was able to see this truth for what it was. It was as if I could see that "the Emperor had no clothes." In other words, my judgment had no validity. It was just a familiar reactive pattern that often surfaced when I was feeling the anticipation of being on stage and watched by others.

From that moment onward in my life, I found it easier to simply recognize when my mind was engaging in judgment. Rather than reacting to my judgments, I steadily became more capable of gently shifting the focus of my awareness from the internal mental noise back to my heart. It's exhilarating to be able to rise above the interference of my mind's narrow concerns.

JUDGMENT VS. EVALUATION

When we negatively judge ourselves in any way for our behavior, the underlying message being communicated is that who we are, at our core, is fundamentally wrong, bad, inadequate or unacceptable. It's straight-up character assassination. This self-indictment is a crime against ourselves. In reality, just because we make a mistake in our process of learning something in our life doesn't make us less worthy. Our worthiness is non-negotiable. In judging ourselves, we fail to make a wise and compassionate distinction between who we are as a person and our behavior.

It's important to recognize that there is a fundamental difference between judgment and evaluation. What comprises judgment is when we strike against the core of who we are by making ourselves wrong. At the same time, of course, we do need to effectively evaluate our and others' behavior and actions in order to keep ourselves safe and make wise, discerning choices. But we can skillfully evaluate our inner and outer world without interweaving negative judgment into the process.

The damaging paradigm and unconscious habit of judgment and shame is instilled in us early in most of our lives through our families, school systems and religious institutions. These hierarchical structures often encourage an abuse of power and unhealthy forms of competitiveness. More often than not, they don't foster empowering, nourishing environments in which everyone can thrive in their uniqueness and beauty with differences being honored and celebrated.

Your Authentic Self knows how to participate in life and evaluate reality in a neutral, wise and discerning way. The essential key, when relating to yourself or others, is making a clear distinction between who we are in our deepest nature as distinct from our momentary thoughts, feelings and behavior. Moving away from judgment gives yourself and others permission to learn. As a human being, you are always learning. And, in a compassionate world, mistakes are an essential part of how we all grow and mature.

THE JUDGE

The inner judge is a negative aspect of our mind solely devoted to criticizing us. It's the voice in our head that is trying in its own way to protect us, yet is never happy with our performance. In the eyes of the judge, who we are is never enough and what we do is always flawed in some way.

The inner judge makes a fundamental mistake by believing that there is legitimacy to an orientation of judgment. The judge believes that somehow it is engaged in a worthwhile venture. The truth is, judgment is never worthwhile. It is always destructive. Neutral evaluation and discernment, on the other hand, are essential as they provide us with an intelligent compass as we navigate our lives.

Ironically, this inner critic is genuinely trying to help us by serving as our protector. Sourced from early traumatic experiences, it wants us to feel safe and doesn't want us to be hurt. In an effort to protect us from the condemnation of others, it discourages us from taking risks and living a larger life led by our Authentic Self. While this mental pattern may have assisted us in surviving when we were younger, later in life it simply induces paralysis. A central principle to keep in mind is that we can relate to our judge in a loving, honorable way.

One simple way to discern the difference between the false self and the Authentic Self is that the false self is attached to the way we have arranged our lives and is fearful of change. This is one fundamental reason why so many of us unconsciously sabotage our efforts at success. Taking on a large project, becoming more accountable, being more visible in the world, or leaving a relationship—all of these are examples of life circumstances which can threaten the security of the false self. This limited identity often makes security its top priority and defines success as making as few changes as possible.

Your Authentic Self, on the other hand, has no attachment to your being any particular way. It is capable of embracing the polarities within you without judging them as either positive or negative. It also has no allegiance to the past and puts no limitations on the future. This deeper self, the real you within, is capable of perceiving different sides of the story and can make choices that honor the protective concerns of your false self while also allowing you to evolve beyond their constraints.

Once your Authentic Self steps forward into its natural leadership role in your consciousness, the inner judge appreciates being recognized for its underlying loyalty. It welcomes being educated into knowing that you are indeed safe and that there is no longer any need to hold judgments. As you anchor your ability to lovingly observe and take dominion over your mind, your inner judge steadily transforms into being a neutral, compassionate and skillful evaluator.

Invitation for Discovery

As you reflect upon your relationship with your inner judge, take some time to consider how all along it has actually been acting in your favor and attempting to support you in moving forward. Enter into a back and forth, free-flowing conversation with your inner judge in which you recognize and appreciate that its criticism of you has been designed to keep you safe. As you open yourself to appreciate this internal alarm system for its loyal efforts on your behalf, give yourself the gift of writing a few words of thanks in your *Journal* for all the ways your inner judge has been steadfastly in your corner.

ACCEPTANCE & COOPERATION

Genuine neutral observation is marked by a deep level of acceptance. Acceptance is a consciousness of unconditional love with no expectations, simply a desire to be uncritically present in the moment just as it is. As we come to accept and appreciate that outer reality often has its own plans and a timing that does not match our hopes and expectations, we begin to relax. We are then able to let go of our mental resistance and stop fighting a war for control that we cannot win—in favor of dancing in an existence marked by safety, ease and joy.

Accepting something without judgment does not mean agreeing with it. It is a process of learning the art of not taking things personally, of giving up our thinking that the world revolves around just us, and letting go of assuming that life should be different than how it is.

COMPASSIONATE SELF-FORGIVENESS

One of the deepest levels of suffering we can carry occurs when we harshly judge ourselves or other people. This is why loving self-forgiveness is essential for healing our suffering. It is an antidote to judgment and involves extending compassion to ourselves. This is a process of bringing tenderness to the parts of us that we have judged as wrong or bad. By doing so, we create a natural bridge back to our love and freedom. When we judge others, we are holding the presence of negative judgment within our own consciousness, and are at the mercy of its destructive energies.

The process of forgiveness is much like making a sincere apology to yourself. Whenever you become aware of a harsh self-judgment, you can say, "Oh, I see what I've done. I've struck against myself with a judgment. I see my error. I'm sorry. I would like to take that back and let it go now." Compassionate forgiveness is the gateway to emotional maturity. The simple power of extending healing energy towards yourself and others is immensely transformative.

Invitation for Discovery

1. I invite you to identify someone in your life who you perceive

as having treated you harshly, someone from whom you still carry a level of hurt or disturbance.

2. As you reflect upon this person and the painful circumstances that played out in your relationship with them, identify any specific negative judgments you are still holding towards them or yourself for how they treated you.

3. Gently acknowledge any painful feelings that still reside within you that are associated with this person.

4. Make a distinction between behavior and essence. Can you see your and their essential beauty regardless of any errors that may have been made?

5. With sincere intention, extend compassion to yourself and this person, allowing your softness to embrace any remaining pain as you re-open your heart.

6. Take a few moments to appreciate this person as a valuable teacher to you, someone who has made a rich contribution to your path of learning and healing.

OUR INNER CHILD

I was 30 years old when, thankfully, the energies of my childlike self surprisingly reawakened and began flowing in wondrous ways through my heart. As I climbed out of my protective shell of unworthiness and released more of the pain I had been carrying, I rediscovered my laughter. It was magical. A large, joyous, boisterous laugh all of a sudden started flowing through me. I began laughing in a distinctive way that people have come to recognize as one of my trademarks.

Soon afterwards, I did some transformational work and connected with my inner child. He let me know his name: Beau. Ever since Beau consciously reappeared in my life, we've been inseparable. He is a spiritual ally and a powerful source of joy, intuition and enthusiasm. Beau likes horsing around, being playful, and taking days off to do nothing. We enjoy being in our body and are nourished by the presence of nature and beauty. We delight in being around people who are also in touch with their childlike flow of energies. My Authentic Self is Beau's finest friend and protector.

Your inner child lives at the core of your Authentic Self. It is an eternally young aspect within you that is innocent, transparent and lives in the moment. Nothing that has happened to you in your life, no matter how horrific, can damage the Spirit of your inner child.

There is a distinct difference between childish and childlike. The psychiatrist, Carl Jung, considered the child archetype to be one of the most powerful aspects of our consciousness. This presence inside us carries wisdom, creativity and unbridled enthusiasm. Some of the most powerful, creative people throughout history have radiated a childlike quality. Abraham Lincoln, Albert Einstein and Oprah Winfrey are some excellent examples. Those who have spent time in their presence consistently describe experiencing a contagious, playful and flowing electricity.

We witness the glory of the inner child when we watch young children play. One moment they might be playing all together and with such joy, then perhaps they get into an argument and begin crying. The next moment they're dancing with each other. Amazingly, they don't hold onto the memory of what happened 5 minutes ago.

For most of us, the primary challenge we have with our inner child is simply not being adequately connected to its signature uniqueness and expression. Somehow along the way, often under the pressure of trauma, criticism and the desire to please others, we consciously let go of its hand and presence in our day-to-day life. With clear intention and consistent investment of time and care, each of us can restore a vibrant relationship with our magical childlike presence.

WINGS

John Daniel Ward

ACT I

I opened a door to a dark closet
and began to remove things
I had discarded from my young life.

The broken rocking horse,
the red wagon with wobbly wheels.
That baseball mitt which always seemed to have a hole in it.

In the corner of the closet,
the darkest corner
sat a dirty flattened pile.

I brought the pile into the light.
Faint memories began to flicker in my mind.

These were wings I had lost long ago,
they were dusty and matted and limp.

I began to open them
but they tore and fell apart in my hands.

Carefully, lovingly,
I began to mend them
feather by feather, stitch by stitch.

I was the mother and the father.
As I touched the wings
I remembered how it felt to fly.

It was so long ago.

ACT II

The voice said "fly".

What do you mean fly?

it's been too long.

This is not a bicycle
these are wings
this is my life.

I tried them on,
they were uncomfortable and stiff.
I was stiff and scared.

I closed my eyes.

I remembered again
how it felt to fly.

The voice yelled "JUMP!"
So, I ran and ran and jumped,
over the edge of my fear.

I began to fall and tumble
out of control.

Somehow through my loving,
the wings caught the wind
and opened up.

I was flying,
I was actually flying.
Soaring.

My heart was full
once again.

As it was so long ago.

Invitation for Discovery

1. Capturing meaningful memories from your childhood will assist you to rekindle your connection with your inner child. Take some time to recall what you most enjoyed doing as a young child and how it made you feel. Was this activity something you did alone or with others? How did your family and friends respond to you while you were engaged with it? What became of this treasured expression? Is it still part of your life, or did it get left behind long ago like the wings in John Ward's poem above?

2. I invite you to ask family members and childhood friends how they experienced you when you were young. Which of your unique qualities and expressions stood out to them? What specific memories of you can they share? As you consciously reminisce about these years, the pure energies of your childlike self may be more accessible to flow through your heart. Record your discoveries and sensations in your *Journal*.

3. Give yourself the gift of writing out an interactive dialogue with your inner child to deepen your connection with one another. One way to approach this kind of writing is to use your non-dominant hand for the child and your dominant hand for your Authentic Self. This technique can also be used for any newly emerging aspect within your consciousness. The reason it's so effective is that the non-dominant hand is connected with the intuitive side of the brain. And because you're probably not as agile in writing with your non-dominant hand, the chances are that what flows through you will be more intuitive and feeling-oriented, the hallmarks of experiencing our inner child.

BIG SUR HEALING

I was traveling with a friend up the California coast. We decided to stop for lunch in Big Sur. We sat overlooking the breathtaking mountains and ocean coastline, a view that is known around the world. During our meal, I perceived our waitress as being pushy, trying to sell us more food so the bill would be larger and thus her tip higher. I felt she was ruining the beautiful time we were having. Inwardly, I was annoyed.

When we got outside the restaurant, knowing I was still emotionally triggered by this woman, I realized it was important to give a voice to my triggered feelings. My friend agreed to hold space and hear me while I sat down on a bench, closed my eyes, and explored my pain. The initial layer of my experience was irritation. Then I realized I had felt offended. This hurt place felt like it had been treated like a credit card rather than a human being, and also felt like she had marred our lunch.

As I allowed myself to drop further into my vulnerability, a much younger aspect of me emerged and started to talk, "I don't like it when people intrude on me, or force themselves on me. I don't like it when they're bigger than me and I feel bullied." And then, a very old memory surfaced, one I was not aware of previously. I reconnected with a scene of me being abused when I was 5 years old. My big brother, Michael, and I were in the shower and he was doing sexual things to me that felt very wrong. He wouldn't stop when I asked him to. I did not want to be there but I was at his mercy and felt helpless.

I allowed this visual memory of being violated to surface. I was tenderly embracing this young child, whom I could see in my imagination, and giving him permission to feel its feelings, to tell me what it remembered. My Authentic Self reassured this little boy, "You did not deserve to be treated that way, and I am grateful you are revealing your pain to me." In my imagination, I held the hand of my child self and placed my arms around him in an embrace, letting him know with gentle words that I loved him and would always protect him. Thankfully, he felt safe enough to cry as he relived the memory and allowed my love in. This bonding between us was profoundly healing.

That same evening, I had a dream. In it, I found myself alone in a dark and cold dungeon just after having been tortured by my captors. My body was in so much pain. It was as if I was visiting another lifetime where I had suffered immensely. I sat in the dark in my dream, terrified that my captors would soon return to continue what they had started. I woke up in terror. It was the waiting for them that was causing me the most anguish, even more than the actual torture. I woke up from the dream breathing heavily and sweating.

I instinctively recognized that this dream was offering an even deeper level of healing related to my inner work about my brother and sexuality from earlier that day. I re-entered the dream experience in my waking state and brought forward the loving and wise presence of my Authentic Self, which held me close as I allowed myself to re-experience the fullness of my terror. Embraced by my own compassion, I, the prisoner, cried and allowed myself to share all my thoughts and feelings. Then, in my imagination, I witnessed us, the one who had been tortured and I, the Authentic Self, walking our way out of the dungeon into safety and freedom.

As we did, I had a powerful insight: that through this dream I was being taken back to the root of the triggering emotions involving the waitress and the memory of my brother, to the very roots of the deep sensitivity that I carry in this lifetime. I was filled with a depth of compassion towards myself that I had not previously known. I forgave myself for the judgments I had placed against myself throughout my life as being "too sensitive," and came into a new level of treasuring the beauty and gift of my own tenderness.

THE HEALING OF MEMORIES

This multi-layered healing process, which unfolded over the course of one day, remains one of the most transformative experiences of my life. Life had given me an opportunity to move deeper into my own healing and integration by revealing a core wound pattern from my unconscious. By consciously and safely allowing myself to experience these painful memories and emotions, the healing energies of my heart were activated and blessed me with profound love.

Following this healing of memories experience, I became much less triggered when people treated me in a way that I did not like. I went from being overreactive at times to having compassion for those who I felt had wronged me. I realized that others are doing the best they can and that their actions towards me aren't personal. I learned that I could find triumph and love in the most challenging of circumstances.

AUTHENTIC SELF DIALOGUE

As reflected in my Big Sur inner work, my Authentic Self skillfully engaged in an inner dialogue with first my 5-year-old self who was abused by my brother, and then with the aspect of me that was haunted by the dream of being tortured. In both instances, my Authentic Self conversed with these inner aspects in much the same way I would counsel with a client. These inner aspects are very much like real people, in that they like to feel that they have our undivided attention. They appreciate being given the time to express themselves and be heard.

In consideration of my past life memories, it is important to note that I've learned that it is not necessary for me to have any beliefs about whether these previous lifetimes have actually taken place or not. It's irrelevant. What is essential is my willingness to honor my experience just as it unfolds from my unconscious. Very simply, these are the images that surfaced in my consciousness requesting to be met, and I met them with love. Whatever inner territory that is naturally emerging in the moment is ripe for our own healing, and is to be embraced with empathy and compassion.

It is important to remain non-judgmental when facilitating this level of inner work, for if our inner aspects sense from us that there is a lack of time, safety or acceptance, they will often withdraw back far enough to remain unseen while still unconsciously steering our behavior. Whenever possible, allow your Authentic Self to reach out to any aspects that are carrying disturbance or feel a need to express themselves. Providing spacious, uninterrupted time for them to emerge is the key to healing and liberation.

An invaluable resource for learning more about this level of inner work is Gestalt Therapy. It was developed by Fritz Perls in the 1950's and focuses on reconnecting with our wholeness by embracing disowned aspects of ourselves. As a pathway for reintegration, one powerful Gestalt tool is to give a voice to those aspects inside that have been abandoned or neglected.

An additional excellent resource is Voice Dialogue, a powerful technique for psychological exploration and integration developed by Hal and Sidra Stone. Given that a range of different selves reside within each of us, Voice Dialogue gives us a chance to recognize, understand and work with these selves in a safe, healing and creative way.

Both of these approaches assist the Authentic Self in establishing a sincere connection and dialogue with our inner choir of voices as, one-by-one, they feel safe to emerge. These distinct aspects can then learn about each other and their respective needs. I utilized each of these powerful approaches when facilitating my multi-layered Big Sur healing journey.

Different people need different things at different times in their journey of growth. Psychotherapy may be needed in instances of severe mental or emotional disturbance, such as when a person feels suicidal, dangerously out of control, or stuck in persistent patterns of behavior that are counterproductive or damaging.

Ongoing therapy can often be an essential component when repairing the damage done by a severely dysfunctional, abusive or alcoholic family. At the same time, therapy is not just for dealing with extreme circumstances and symptoms. The one-on-one therapeutic process can be an invaluable way of touching into our rich inner life and coming into greater levels of fulfillment and aliveness.

The need to heal our inner world is a call to action for which it seems the very destiny of humanity relies upon us answering. By learning to honor the multiplicity of our selves, we can consciously achieve greater levels of inner peace and maturity in our inner world, our close relationships, and within the communities that surround us.

"The privilege of a lifetime is becoming who you truly are."

~ Carl Jung

Invitation for Discovery

1. I invite you to identify a recent time in your life when you were emotionally triggered by someone. As you reflect upon this situation, set up 2 chairs directly facing each other to facilitate a dialogue. One chair is designated as the chair where your Authentic Self sits, while the other chair is for the aspect inside of you that's been emotionally triggered. It's astonishing how easy and powerful it can be to engage a dialogue between your Authentic Self and an aspect that's upset by simply giving them each a voice and having them speak back and forth with each other in real time.

2. I invite you to start the dialogue process by sitting in the chair designated for the aspect you want to converse with. Allow this aspect that is upset to share briefly and honestly with the Authentic Self, then physically switch chairs and allow your Authentic Self to speak back to the aspect that is upset, carefully responding to the specifics that it just shared. For perhaps 10-15 minutes, making

sure you switch chairs as the Authentic Self and the aspect listen to and respond to each other, continue the dialogue until both are complete with what they want to express. A spacious and honorable dialogue builds understanding and greater teamwork between your Authentic Self and the aspect that is facing a challenge.

While it may initially feel awkward to open an inner dialogue like this, if you stay with it a sense of ease and comfort often emerges. This is actually a natural process, as we all have a wide range of different aspects residing in our consciousness. New discoveries and insights often reveal themselves in this dialogue process with the Authentic Self. Feelings get expressed with safety, questions get asked and answered, and our deeper needs can finally get expressed and met.

By engaging in this inner work, you will never be alone again. You will always have a partner walking through life with you that is caring, dynamic and real. All that's required for this inner partnership to develop is a willingness to enter into heartfelt dialogue with your Authentic Self in a consistent way over time. Your inner aspects can move from living in relative isolation in your unconscious into an honest, safe and conscious relationship with your Authentic Self. Lovingly embracing the multiplicity of selves within our consciousness is a gateway to the experience of wholeness and the Divine.

FINDING BOTTLES

"We are finding bottles at the bottom of the ocean. All the time. We mean to say that there are parts of ourselves buried so far away from ourselves that they are hidden. But there comes a time when the heart must speak, the heart must open and the earlier parts of ourselves, the child inside of us, must be released, must stand at the edge of the ocean and have her say. She must be born. It's the act of healing: to incorporate all the wounded parts of ourselves, to love them."

An excerpt from a conversation about writing the poem "I found a bottle at the bottom of the ocean," written by Alicia Elkort and Jenn Givhan, both published in *The Georgie Review*.

CHAPTER 10

Embracing Death as Our Sacred Companion

"It is not length of life, but depth of life."
~ Ralph Waldo Emerson

A PARTING GIFT

"Dad, I need your help. I don't know what to do. I just gave you an extra dose of morphine by mistake." It was the middle of the night, and I uttered these words remembering there would be frightening repercussions for my father if given too much morphine. I felt helpless seeing him out of control with terrifying hallucinations when over-medicated, which had happened once before. He hated the feeling, and my error would cause him to experience that again.

My dad was my life. He meant everything to me. I hurt when he hurt. I was handling the night shift again because I wanted to be by his side in these last days of his life. I was in charge of his pain medication. I felt blessed that he could be at home under hospice care during his last days, but it was a big responsibility. If I gave him too little morphine, he was in excruciating physical pain. In my exhaustion from being up most of the last 3 nights, I accidentally gave him an additional pill, forgetting that I had just given him one. My heart was already breaking, given he was near death, and I despaired, "Now this?"

My dad, who had been drifting in and out of consciousness, heard my confession about giving him his medication twice. He opened his eyes and said, "I understand. If you could just help me out of bed." At this point in his illness, he was so weak that he hadn't left his bed for days. Slowly, I helped him to the edge of the bed. I didn't know what he was doing, but he insisted on crawling on his knees to the bathroom. When he reached the toilet, he put his finger down his throat and made himself throw up the morphine pill I had just given him. Then, ever so slowly, he crawled back to bed.

I sobbed as I helped my dad back into his bed. As I tucked him in, I told him again how sorry I was. When he caught his breath, he said gently, "Don't worry about it, son, it's okay. It's no problem." I was so moved by my father and his love. Here he was dying, and not only did he have the wherewithal to solve this problem, but his tender concern was for relieving my anguish. It was one of the kindest gifts anyone had ever given me. He went on, still breathless, "We all make mistakes. It's all right, we got it." He was so pure and innocent in that moment. It just blew me away. He then slipped into unconsciousness and calmly died a few hours later. Those were the final words between me and my dad.

"Sometimes the smallest things take
up the most room in your heart."

~ Winnie-the-Pooh

THE FIERCE REALITY

Woven within every spiritual tradition is an understanding that death is always at our side. While for many the inevitability of physical death is terrifying, for others it is not. The awareness of our mortality has a way of stripping away the trivial and assisting us in looking at ourselves and the world with astonishing freshness. This mysterious eventuality leaves us no place to hide. Most importantly, it is possible to learn to embrace our mortality in a way that ushers us into living more fully.

Everyone who comes face-to-face with their physical departure has to find a way to reckon with this reality, as my father did. He was an extraordinarily dedicated man who had served in the infantry in the Korean War. He told me he had witnessed a lot of horrific things in the war, but he never wanted to talk about them. I asked him once if he had ever witnessed anyone being killed in the war, and he simply nodded his head yes. There were no words...his silence spoke volumes. He was quite convinced when he was in Korea that he would not return home alive. When, at last, he safely stepped off the ship in the San Diego harbor, he kissed the ground with relief and gratitude. From that point on, he was immensely grateful for the smallest things in life, and his 19-year dance with cancer only made him appreciate the gift of life all the more.

Given that my dad's cancer journey began when I was in my teens, I encountered the prospect of physical death and its profound teachings early in my life. I learned that everything is dissolving constantly, inwardly and outwardly, and that we are all in a perpetual process of death and birthing new life. I discovered how closely grief and beauty, as well as pain and joy, are interwoven. This perspective helped me cherish all the days of my dad's life—and more fully appreciate being alive in my own skin. For most of my life I have referred to death as my sacred companion, for it has beautifully honed me towards wholehearted living.

The fierce reality is that we will either be saying goodbye to everyone we know and care for—or they will be saying goodbye to us. One of us will go first. Life is designed this way. As we grow older, there comes an increasing recognition that our body doesn't have an indefinite time on this earth. Indeed a time will arrive when we will close our eyes and not open them again. In his book, *The Last Year of My Life*, Stephen Levine speaks to the power of perpetually approaching our life by remembering that it comes to an end—an attitude that serves as a gateway to greater aliveness.

BRAVE CONVERSATIONS

Interestingly, the Authentic Self isn't concerned with death. It isn't even concerned about everything being over at the end of our lives. But it does want to live the greatest adventure that it can in this lifetime.

Over the years, I have supported many clients in the midst of terminal illness who have been facing the last months and weeks of their lives. Invariably, as the end nears, coming to peace with loved ones often becomes paramount to them.

Completing unfinished business involves entering into brave conversations that allow a depth of love and truth to come front and center. Often, even after years of disturbance and separation, walls in these core relationships come down and rich healing occurs. With this in mind, a most essential question emerges, "Why wait until we are dying to have these brave conversations?"

By consciously reminding ourselves that this year, or even this day, may be our last—for in reality, we never know—we are afforded an opportunity to address all aspects of our lives with full care and attention. This can be profoundly motivating. As we recognize that we have been supremely gifted with our human incarnation, the central question becomes our guide each day, "What do we want to make of the gift of our life?"

"Death never takes the wise by surprise.
They are always ready to go."
~ Jean de La Fontaine

GATHERING WISDOM

"For Octogenarians Only!" While preparing for one of my transformational workshops, we put this sign on 2 comfy, supportive chairs in our circle. My wife's parents, Bob and Mary Lou, who were then in their 80's, were active participants in this 11-month Sacred Passages program I was facilitating which was held one weekend per month. We sought to honor them as elders of the community.

Bob and Mary Lou were like my second parents. I was blessed to feel close to each of them like I was with my mom and dad. They were vital, open-hearted, and carried a contagious humility and generosity. Thankful for the gift of life and each other, they had been married for over 60 years at the time, and were the embodiment of wise elders.

We felt it was a privilege to cherish them in any way we could, from transportation to special accommodations. While they were sitting on the luxurious "throne" chairs we provided, taking in all the love we offered them, every month they gave us the gift of overflow from their hearts. Given their playfulness and connection with their childlike selves, in many ways we experienced them as the youngest members of our group

As part of the program, Bob and Mary Lou each wrote and self-published a wisdom-

laced book about their lives, a dream they each had been holding for decades. They had a wealth of stories to tell. Mary Lou had grown up as a child of missionaries in Cameroon, Africa and was a licensed psychotherapist. Bob was an ordained minister throughout his life and also held a PhD in Gestalt Therapy. Their transparent sharing about their youth, growing old together and how they embraced their mortality was always refreshing. They blessed all who crossed their path and served as remarkable role models for conscious aging.

HONORING ELDERS

It is a rare gift to encounter someone in the later years of life who is not only connected with their inner Light, but who also approaches the reality of physical death with their hearts wide open. Bob and Mary Lou were such people.

As we grow older, we don't need to be diminished by the inevitable losses that accompany the passage of time. We carry priceless accumulated life experiences and deserve to be respected for the ways we have evolved and for the wisdom we have gained along the way. Bob and Mary Lou taught me by example that legacy is the natural by-product of a well-lived life.

A vibrant elder refers to someone who has immersed themselves in an authentic life and now carries a presence of wisdom and nobility. They've harvested their life experiences and naturally share their treasures with others.

In our Western culture, we generally avoid facing the reality of death and often view aging and elders as a liability. Those late in their life are viewed as no longer productive or desirable members of society because we place such a high premium upon outer performance and appearance. It's rare to find a community in the West that honors the aged, yet thankfully there are cultures around the world that celebrate elders as vital members of their community.

The final stage of psychologist Eric Erikson's well-known psychosocial stages of development centers upon aging and the theme of creative contribution. At best, this stage of life is free of many outer responsibilities and makes deeper levels of fulfillment available as elders share from a place of overflow as they contribute to the lives of others.

Invitation for Discovery

1. I invite you to identify an older person in your life who has been an inspiration to you. What inner qualities did this wise elder possess, and what specific actions did they take that stirred and encouraged you to be a better version of yourself?

2. If they are still alive, consider reaching out to them and expressing your thanks for who they are and their impact upon your life.

GRIEF HAS ITS WAY

I had never known this level of loss. Even though the fear of my dad dying was with me for almost 2 decades, he had still been there. Then he died, and I was devastated beyond comprehension.

Profound grief rolled through me. I wailed. I missed him. I would have done anything to hold his hand just one more time, but I couldn't. Grief was having its way with me, and somehow I intuitively knew that I needed to allow it. Someone shared with me at the time that the depth of our grief is equivalent to the depth of our love, and I felt this truth in my bones.

As part of my mourning process, I found myself reflecting back on many powerful experiences I had shared with my father. About 2 months prior to his passing, before he became too ill to enjoy company, I had organized a celebration of life gathering to honor him. During the gathering, each person shared precious memories of my dad, beginning with those who had known him since he was a young boy and progressing through each decade of his life. My father and everyone in attendance were so moved as the arc of his life became illuminated in their touching stories. We had shared so much richness together since he was first told he would not live long, and he ended up defying those odds for 19 years. We had made every moment count.

After he died, as part of my grieving process, I watched the video of his life celebration to once again partake of the radiance of his one-of-a-kind heart. Over and over again, I reflected upon the eve of his passing, when I was sitting on the edge of his bed and holding his hand. On that last night, we reminisced about riding motorcycles and going to college together. My dad then reached over and placed his hand softly on my heart. It was like he was transmitting a communication from the center of his being to the center of mine, and as tears rolled down his cheeks he said, "Son, be sure to appreciate every day. Every day." In this bittersweet moment, underneath these words was also the sentiment, "I know I won't be there to enjoy it with you any longer." We cried and cried…

With this poignant exchange, my father impressed upon me a visceral reminder that I could be gone at any time—thus the importance of daily appreciating and treasuring the gift of life.

"Those we love never truly leave us.
There are things that death cannot touch."
~ Jack Thorne

THE LIFTING OF THE SHADOW

I was lying on my bed, crying and pining for my dad. Susan, with so much love, gently sat down next to me and spoke to me from her heart, "You know, darling, I have an intuition. It's been almost a month now since your dad died, and it may be wise for you to consider that it is time to let him go."

I heard these simple words and was struck by her wisdom. I knew she was right. I realized at that moment that as bountiful as my years of living with my dad had been, there would always be a part of me that felt like I didn't get enough time with him.

I placed my hands on my heart, just as my father had done for me in the hours before his passing, and said out loud, "I'm going to let go of you, Dad, instead of trying to hold on." As I did, the presence of grief lifted and a profound sense of peace flowed through me. At that moment, it felt like he moved from being an outside presence to an inside presence, which deeply comforted me.

The next weekend, Susan and her daughter, Alaya, and my mother and I traveled to the Mojave desert where my father had cherished riding his motorcycles. We silently spread his ashes over the land. We closed by sharing some of our favorite memories of him before traveling home.

"The song is ended, but the melody lingers on."
~ Irving Berlin

The death of my dad was a sacred passage in my life. Although he died in 1990, to this day I continue to have real and meaningful conversations with him inside myself. I see his signature reflected in many of the ways I choose to live my life, and thank him regularly for his towering contribution. Whenever I am called in my heart to reach out his way, his abiding love and encouragement is always present and available.

Invitation for Discovery

I invite you to identify someone you've lost in your life for whom you still carry some measure of unresolved grief. What steps might you take to support yourself in lifting the shadow? Some possibilities include writing an intimate letter to them and keeping it to re-read from time to time, or having an inner dialogue with them, or perhaps placing a photograph of them in your home where you'll see it regularly and can call them into your heart. Capture your process in your *Journal.*`

WIDE OPEN

by Dawna Markova

I will not die an unlived life.
I will not live in fear
of falling or catching fire.
I choose to inhabit my days,
to allow my living to open me,
to make me less afraid,
more accessible;
to loosen my heart
until it becomes a wing,
a torch, a promise.
I choose to risk my significance,
to live so that which came to me as seed
goes to the next as blossom,
and that which came to me as blossom
goes on as fruit.

"There is a special quality of stillness in a person
who encounters their shadow wholeheartedly.
Your body may relax in their company because
it understands, in the subtle communications
of their presence, that nothing is excluded
in themselves, or you, from belonging.
Such a person, who has given up guarding
against the shadow, who has come to
wear their scars with dignity, no longer squirms
from discomfort or bristles at suffering.
They no longer brace in avoidance of conflict.
They carry a deep willingness to dance with the
inconstancy of life. They've given up distancing
as a strategy, and made vulnerability an ally."

~ Toko-pa Turner

CHAPTER 11

Appreciating Darkness & Suffering as Divine Messengers

"One does not become enlightened by imagining figures of light, but by making the darkness conscious."

~ Carl Jung

THE LIGHT & THE DARK

I once had a dream that I was walking through a dark and narrow hallway. It was nearly impossible to see. There were many closed doors on both sides of the hallway. A strip of light appeared underneath one of them, and I asked myself, "If I open this door, will the light from the room shine into the dark hallway, or will the darkness from the hallway flow into the lighted room?" To discover the answer, as the dream closed, I turned the handle and opened the door…

This experience occurred in my late 20's, and symbolized to me the reality that the Light is always more powerful than the dark. All of us walk through dark hallways of experience at times, yet underneath it all, it is Light that resides in and emanates from our core. This love and truth inside each of us, our Authentic Self, shines into the darkness to guide our way.

This Light is also our ultimate authority. The more we let go of our conditioning and shadow patterns, the more its radiant presence grants us Divine sovereignty in our consciousness.

CANCER RETURNS

Following our marriage, Susan and I had 2 children together, Johnny and Christian. When the boys were 9 and 7 years old, Susan was diagnosed with stage 4 breast cancer. Threatened with the real possibility of death in her early 50's, she and our family walked through the process of her in-depth treatment, including a mastectomy, radiation and chemotherapy.

I was, of course, quite familiar with cancer and all that comes with it. Like my father, Susan walked her path with bravery and an unwavering dedication to her healing and full recovery. I remember the day, about one week following her first chemotherapy treatment, when she gathered Johnny and Christian and me around her in our kitchen. She had an electric hair clipper in her hand. As she sat down in the chair, she explained to the boys that one of the side effects of her chemotherapy treatments was that all of her hair would be falling out. So, as a sacred ritual, before her hair fell out, she invited them each to remove all of the hair on either side of her head with the clipper, leaving a short mohawk in the center. They did this with glee. After they were finished, she shaved the left and right sides of her head smooth with a razor. She then took out some makeup and made colorful streaks high on her cheek bones so that she looked like a fierce indigenous warrior woman. She was so joyful in this process that she exuded an energy the boys captured and rode on. It was a one-of-a-kind healing ceremony in our family's life.

As Susan was facing the real possibility of dying, and we did not know whether her extensive cancer treatment would be successful, we decided to envision success and encouraged the boys to focus on her journey of healing and wellness. Why feed their fear of possibly losing their mom? As it turned out, although Susan's body took a major toll from her year-long treatment, her cancer went into remission and never returned. My respect and admiration for Susan and her indomitable spirit grew as she fiercely and tenderly navigated her healing passage.

Following her recovery, now determined more than ever to move forward on her lifelong dream of sharing her gifted angelic voice, Susan triumphantly created a CD of her sacred original music called Cradled in Love: Lullabies for Everyone.

SURRENDERING TO OUR JOURNEY

As the experience of more freedom and power emerges in our lives, there are also life experiences that call us to accept our very real human limitations. During these times, we have to come to grips with the fact that we are far less in control of ourselves and the world around us than we would like to think. Susan was not only facing cancer, she was facing the vulnerability of her own mortality.

Life is so profound that it often interweaves freedom and limitation, strength and weakness, all at the same time. Acceptance of our weakness leads to finding our true strength, for when we surrender to what we cannot control, peace arises and we cease to waste our energy on futile resistance.

As suffering is something we all go through, we can support each other as painful circumstances move through our lives. The wisdom we gain from dealing with loss, illness or heartbreak gives us access to the essence of our humanity. Said another way, our challenges and wounding experiences often provide us greater access to the powerful Light we carry within.

Walking through the process of life-threatening cancer can be transformational, no matter the outer result. Meeting suffering from the level of the Authentic Self involves having the strength of heart to bear the pain of the illness as we also hold the faith that we will come out the other side. It involves being vulnerable enough to allow ourselves to cycle through the full range of our feelings with total permission to experience them all. This is the opportunity that such challenges provide. The ability to surrender to what is far beyond our control—including an acceptance of loss, pain and inevitable change—can go hand in hand. Among the many priceless gifts we gain through these passages are greater inner strength, resilience and compassion.

Invitation for Discovery

I invite you to describe in your *Journal* a time in your life when you walked through a difficult challenge. Take a moment to honor yourself for the way you stepped forward as best as you could to support yourself and those around you. What were some of the unexpected gifts and uplifting experiences this challenge brought your way?

DENYING MY HUMANITY

For the first 10 years after opening to my divinity and relationship with Spirit, I found myself striving to be happy, to always be "in the Light." I loved being spiritually high, which I hadn't experienced since the time I was flourishing at age 10. It was wonderful to finally taste it again. This experience became my continual pursuit. I saw myself as "evolved" if I went for long periods in which I didn't experience upset, darkness, or depression. I viewed this as desirable and evidence that I was worthy.

Over time, however, I realized that I was running from something. I was expending considerable energy denying and pushing away my own pain and humanity. I gradually recognized that each life has its own distinctive cycles. At times, my life was rich and flowing, at other times I was traversing a passage that was painful and challenging. This is how it works. Like an ocean tide, my authentic life was a natural ebb and flow of darkness and Light.

BRINGING THE LIGHT TO OUR DARKNESS

It is essential to accept suffering as a core quality of being human, as the Light and dark aspects of our human experience yearn to be accepted and embraced equally. We are all, individually and collectively, on a healing journey designed to expand the range of this embrace. We arrive in this world without a map and throughout our lives face immense challenges and opportunities. We are all learning as we go, and each of us needs all the love and support we can get from each other along the way.

It requires great strength, awareness and skill to remain conscious when we experience suffering. In these dark periods, our Authentic Self can become the unifying source for learning how to hold an accepting, sacred space for ourselves and our journey. It could be referred to as "the Light hidden in the darkness," for it is in the midst of pain and struggle that we often turn to the Divine energies inside that are expressed as compassion and wisdom.

The higher purpose of the Light is actually to bring healing to the places of darkness and pain we encounter in our consciousness. The word heal comes from whole. The darkness and edges of our consciousness are where the real healing occurs, and it is often in the midst of our suffering that we gain access to new levels of wholeness and renewal. I witnessed this growing up with my parents and siblings, as each of us became stronger at our broken places.

The only way that darkness has power over us is when we unwittingly give ourselves over to its presence. Indeed, most destructive actions on this planet take place through unconscious behavior. My brother is an example of someone who, as a result of unhealed trauma from being abused when he was young, gave over to an unconscious pattern of hatred and retribution. The severe disconnect from his Authentic Self was accompanied by overwhelming shame. Then in prison, of all places, he radically transformed the course of his life by opening to a direct experience of Divine, unconditional love. This enabled him to enter into self-forgiveness and by so doing, to lead his life from that point forward in a consciousness of love.

Aspects of ourselves are often pushed into our unconscious, the shadow dimension beyond our conscious awareness, because we judge them as unacceptable. Whenever we reject any aspect of ourselves, we create inner separation and disturbance. This process only fuels our destructive, unconscious patterns.

We may, for example, find ourselves utterly bewildered by how we could be so cruel to a loved one. How could we say such mean-spirited things that cut them to their core? The answer is that there's something unresolved deep within us that's driving our reactive, destructive behavior. Until we become conscious of and heal such patterns, they will direct our lives.

A lot of what is referred to in the therapeutic community as "shadow work" involves consciously acknowledging and making peace with aspects of ourselves that we've rejected. We can learn to live beyond our tendency to judge ourselves, other people, and situations as right or wrong, or good or bad. Over time, both the pattern and the judgments may lose their strength. We are all capable of bringing our shadow aspects out of the darkness where they've been hidden, and shining the healing Light of acceptance upon them.

"Until you make the unconscious conscious,
it will direct your life and you will call it fate."
~ Dr. Carl Jung

Invitation for Discovery

1. I invite you to identify one of your behaviors that you have a tendency to judge as being unacceptable. Capture in your *Journal* the specific ways this behavior plays out in your life, as well as the nature of your harsh judgments toward it.

2. You might consider that your judgments only drive this aspect of your life underground, which breeds a sense of separation and creates unnecessary pain. Might you be willing to simply change your mind and bring forward an attitude of acceptance and compassion for this behavior and all the judgment it has had to endure? Might there be a way to build a healthy relationship with it? In other words, the way to overcome unhealthy behavioral patterns is not to condemn them, but to appreciate that they developed long ago out of an intention to protect you—and to embrace them with love. By being at greater peace with it, you will be more capable of transcending your unconscious patterns and begin making more conscious, constructive choices.

3. Now, take a moment to imagine that you are facing a circumstance in your life that would typically elicit your old behavior. Then, picture and describe yourself responding in a manner that feels more compassionate and supportive.

THE JOY OF FAMILY

I was standing in our backyard, holding a copy of the book, To Kill a Mockingbird. I was reading passages from the book out loud to Christian and Johnny, who were high above me, hanging out on the thick limbs of a gorgeous oak tree, entranced by the story.

I had taken the lead in facilitating homeschooling, and both boys were flourishing with the freedom and organic flow of our learning process. Some kids simply learn better up in trees!

In one year, Johnny amazingly progressed through 6 grade levels of math, and discovered it to be his passion. In a similar, organic way, Christian found his own passion, acting, which he was now exploring up in the tree. As if in the midst of a play, standing atop the mast of a ship, he excitedly called out to us, "Ahoy, mates. Here she comes!"

At that moment, my 20 year-old step-daughter, Alaya, showed up to greet us. She smiled and asked, "What classic are you reading today?"

The boys adored her. Alaya was a natural born leader with a heartfelt desire to serve others. She was home from college, and her presence always filled our family with Light.

There in the backyard, with the sun shining, the 4 of us smiled at each other as we heard Susan inside the house, performing her melodious vocal exercises. A member of a local chorale group, she was preparing for a concert that evening. Her voice was angelic.

After 7 years of homeschooling, the boys returned to public school to finish their education and things continued to go well for them. Johnny was an A+ student and soon had a clear goal of earning a PhD in Engineering. He was on the school track team and was well liked by his peers. Christian had successfully played roles in a wide range of Shakespeare plays in our community.

A SUDDEN FALL

Three years after returning to public schooling, I was driving home from an appointment when I received an urgent call from Johnny's high school counselor. She relayed that Johnny, totally out of character, had yelled at a teacher in front of the entire classroom. He was being suspended. As we would soon learn, his mental health struggles had begun.

Around the same time that Johnny's challenges were unfolding, Susan and I found ourselves sitting in the living room, shaking our heads in despair. We had just found out that Christian had missed 4 days of school. He had recently expressed to us that he was facing challenges in some of his junior high school classes. We walked up to his bedroom to talk to him about this and opened the door. Susan screamed. Christian was sitting on the edge of the bed, holding a razor blade and lacerating deep slices into his forearms. We soon discovered that this was a common teen reaction to severe depression, and was called "cutting." Christian's years-long challenge with symptoms of bipolar disorder was now underway.

A FIRESTORM

Over the next 5 years, Susan and I learned firsthand with our 2 sons how mental illness and drug abuse can decimate a family. We educated ourselves about the realities of teen onset mental illness, a genetic condition whose symptoms arrive suddenly—seemingly out of nowhere—and often lead to a downward spiral. We learned that a large percentage of teens facing mental health issues resort to drugs in a desperate attempt to have, even for brief periods, an experience of relief and a sensation of wholeness. This was certainly the case for both of our boys. In addition to being a destructive beast all on its own, drug addiction exacerbated Christian's bipolar disorder symptoms exponentially, resulting in a tragic and destructive cycle that would last years. It was a harrowing journey for all four of us.

Susan and I reached out for professional support. In support of Christian, we worked closely with psychiatrists, explored his compatibility with a wide range of psychiatric drugs and therapists, and enrolled him in various special education and rehabilitation programs. Despite everything we did, his unraveling continued. It was emotionally exhausting and depleted our financial savings. We were going into debt. We learned that we were not alone, that the circumstances we were facing as a family were far more common than we knew. It felt like we were in the midst of a forest fire that was burning all the way to the sea.

A DESPERATELY NEEDED REVELATION

In the throes of overwhelm and hopelessness, one day I found myself asking Spirit for its strength and guidance. Thankfully, in response to my sincere prayers, inwardly I received the following clear words of revelation, "If you begin to relate to all that will be unfolding within your family as anything but a gift from Spirit, you will be off course." This higher perspective made all the difference for me. It spoke to my Authentic Self and the truth that I could look for and find the blessings occurring in the midst of our cataclysmic circumstances. Again and again, this wisdom assisted me in shifting my energies beyond a state of feeling victimized. From that point forward, I endured by becoming a student of misfortune, dedicated to learning and being strengthened by all that was unfolding.

WEATHERING THE STORM

Much like when I was a teenager and tried to do everything I could for my mom and dad, I once again found myself compelled to try and be the hero in our family. I strove with all my might to rescue Johnny and Christian in any way imaginable. This, much to my surprise, was the adaptive pattern of my false self that had become prominent in my teens when I had attempted to rescue both of my parents from their own pain.

Johnny's life crumbled as his depression continually worsened. He could no longer perform at a high level academically. Even with all the assistance we provided, he was barely able to finish his senior year classes with passing grades. Almost all of his friends pulled away from him. He was lost, and our attempts at securing successful treatment were not helping him.

Despite our valiant efforts to support his healing and well-being, Christian's anxiety and depression deepened, and the serious nature of his self-destructive behaviors increased. The use of drugs exacerbated his problems, and suicide attempts became a standard feature of our lives. Keeping Christian alive became our overriding objective. His entrenched drug addiction only made him more unstable, steadily eroding his self-esteem and any sense of a promising future.

Susan and I received excellent professional guidance, and gradually recognized that there was actually a clear distinction between supporting our children and attempting to rescue them. We learned specific ways that we were engaging in unhealthy, codependent behaviors as parents. We had to learn the importance of establishing firm boundaries regarding no drug use while our sons lived in the house. To not do so was, in fact, enabling them. I had to steadily wean myself away from trying to be the hero who thought he could rescue them by solving all their problems.

Susan and I had become over-responsible and oversteering as parents. We had entered into an unconscious pattern of leading our lives from the fearful voice of our false selves. We realized that a huge source of our exhaustion was due to neglecting ourselves and each other.

Steady therapeutic assistance supported us in facing and letting go of our fears. We accepted the fact that we weren't superhuman, that we had our own needs, and we needed to take much better care of ourselves. I slowly returned to the safety and solid ground of my

Authentic Self, and thankfully discovered a way through the fire. I once again began taking great care of my body, recommitted to a disciplined meditation practice, and turned my creative energies toward nourishing and rebuilding my private practice.

Ever so slowly, we witnessed the boys making the most progress on their own paths when we stopped trying to rescue them and instead, let them face their own pain and consequences. As they learned to take greater responsibility for their choices, both boys turned towards a healthier future.

Thankfully, after facing 3 years of sustained trauma, the doctors discovered that Johnny had a unique and rare brain chemistry in which the use of even small amounts of marijuana caused severe depression. With this discovery, he simply stopped using marijuana and began stabilizing. Over the next few months, he returned to his healthy, fully functioning self. He was incredibly relieved to have a promising life back in his hands. Grateful beyond measure, he triumphantly resurrected his friendships, and resumed pursuing his educational and professional goals.

A MOST UNEXPECTED ENDING

All these years of trauma with the boys and our family tore at our marriage. Susan and I discovered that having even one child with significant mental illness and substance abuse puts an extraordinary strain on a marriage—often causing even the healthiest of them to fracture and come to an end. Years of frustration and exhaustion in these extreme circumstances take their toll, and judgment and blame commonly erode spousal communications.

As we approached our 25th year together, the strain on our marriage mounted. Despite extensive marriage counseling, the depth of pain and loneliness in the relationship continued to grow. As much as Susan and I loved each other, through all the heartache we were enduring with Johnny and Christian, fundamental differences emerged between us in how best to support them as they were engulfed in their troubles. These differences drove a painful wedge between us which, in the end, proved fatal to our marriage.

In the final months, I entered a process of deep reflection about my commitment to our marriage, which included bravely honest conversations with myself and Susan. Up until this point, I had never even considered the possibility of us not remaining together. One day I was shocked when I had the thought, "Is this partnership really working for my own well-being and the overall health of everyone in our family?" It felt blasphemous and dangerous to even raise the question. I'm a loyal person, and realized that after being together for decades, I had been assuming for quite some time that Susan and I would be married until the end of our lives.

As I was reckoning with the guilt I had about the possibility of leaving a long-term marriage, a powerful recollection surfaced from 25 years earlier that gifted me with insight and healing. Susan and I were each on a deep spiritual path when we got married. At that time, as we composed our wedding vows, neither of us was aligned with the commitment of, "until death do us part." The foundation of our commitment to each other rested upon each of us being steadily true to ourselves and to Spirit's guidance within us. Thus, while we both shared a vision of being together for the whole of our lives, our sacred vow was to only stay married as long as each of us had an unquestionable knowing that remaining together was still aligned within our hearts. This recollection from the very roots of our marriage allowed me to release the judgment towards myself that I was being disloyal. It also provided me the sacred space to honor the voice of my Soul, whose sincere desire was to serve me and each member of my family in the highest way.

I was utterly shocked that our marriage could be ending. I fought against this possibility. For well over a year, we tried to resurrect our marriage with the assistance of 2 highly qualified therapists. This encounter with the intention of bridging our pain and differences was to no avail.

At this juncture, I dared to turn towards my Authentic Self. I had to connect with and act on the truth of my heart. One day I wrote out the following question in my journal: "Is my heart truly committed to continuing to build my life with Susan?" After listening for some time, the answer from the well of truth inside me revealed itself in the following words: "Absolutely not, and you haven't been for a couple of years." This knowing came in loud and clear, and I knew it to be true. In my experience with my Authentic Self, when I connect with this level of profound revelation, it isn't something that's negotiable. It wasn't even a decision—it was an inner spiritual directive that I was being asked to surrender to and cooperate with. Thus, to have stayed in the marriage would have been Self-betrayal, and would have also betrayed the essence of my vows as a partner. Not only did a deep voice within me call for this change, I knew that embodying Light with greater integrity was also the best way that I could serve myself, Susan and our children.

I summoned the strength to go to Susan, look directly in her eyes and tell her, "I love you and will always love you, but my heart is no longer aligned with continuing to build our lives together. I'm very, very sorry." We both wept. She was crushed, as she had wanted to remain married until the end of our lives. In the midst of our immense and mutual grief, I initiated the process of honorably and sensitively dismantling our marriage and moving on to the next season of my life's expression. This included selling our beautiful home and addressing all the financial and legal issues between us. I never imagined that I would be divorced. I discovered for myself how profoundly everyone in a family suffers in a divorce. It was a most fierce and tender sacred passage for us all.

BLESSED BY HARDSHIP

Our lives can be blessed by hardship and suffering. If we are willing to be true to ourselves, the revelations we have during our most difficult passages can open us up to new levels of freedom. If we support ourselves during our darkest hours, we get more rooted in the strength of our inner resilience and compassion.

Despite facing formidable shock and grief, from the moment my Authentic Self conveyed to me my truth about the marriage, I found myself at peace. As a result of having walked through this dark passage in our marriage and family with my heart as open as possible, I was astonished to discover that I had matured emotionally and spiritually in significant ways. I had become more firmly anchored in my own strength.

During this passage in our family's journey, there were a number of major fires in Southern California near where we lived, with thousands of people losing their homes. In the midst of these tragic losses, it was heartening to see how people stepped forward with remarkable levels of compassion and generosity in support of those who had lost everything. It was a touching testament to the depth of humanity that becomes available when we support each other in and through our pain. Those in loss who receive this love find that it assists them in being able to go on, to rise to the occasion, and to prevail.

"Compassion is not a relationship between the healer and the wounded.
It's a relationship between equals. Only when we know our own
darkness well can we be present with the darkness of others.
Compassion becomes real when we recognize our shared humanity."

~ Pema Chodron

Whether it is losing a marriage, our home being damaged in a natural disaster, facing major illness, a family member struggling with substance abuse, etc.—invariably each of us at some stage in our lives traverses a major life challenge that includes darkness and suffering. These fierce passages are an essential part of our life curriculum for they grant us blessings that would otherwise elude us.

Scientists discovered long ago that certain vegetation only grows after a forest fire. It doesn't show up any other way. The phrase, "we can become strong at the broken places," recognizes the resilience of the human Spirit that rises during painful circumstances. We can't change the fact that fires happen and bring immense loss in their wake, but we are each capable of responding to suffering and hardship by opening to the opportunity for healing and building new levels of inner strength.

THE GIFTS OF DEPRESSION

Anyone who has been through divorce knows the torture this sacred passage can contain. After almost 3 decades of marriage, I was fully exposed to the depth of grief and depression that accompanied this process.

I've learned that in order to live a truly fulfilling and authentic life, we must develop a respect for the beneficial contribution that depression can bring to our depth as human beings. Melancholy gives the Authentic Self an opportunity to express a unique side of its nature that is as valid as any other, yet we often hide from its gifts because of our distaste for darkness and pain. Depression grants us the opportunity to view our lives from a whole new perspective, thus allowing us to discern things that were previously unseen.

The Authentic Self recognizes the value of human suffering. It knows that depth and revelation uniquely make themselves accessible during challenging times. Depressing thoughts and feelings have a way of carving out an interior space where wisdom can take up residence. In learning to bring radical acceptance to our own pain, we support ourselves in coming into greater levels of emotional and spiritual maturity.

Because of its painful emptiness, it is tempting to look for a way to avoid depression. Yet, entering into its moods and thoughts with an orientation of curiosity can actually be deeply gratifying. Entering into the void where our pain resides assists us in moving beyond accustomed ways of understanding and identifying who we are. Spiritual liberation can find us in these depths.

Denying and hiding our dark places results in a loss of intimacy with ourselves and others, while allowing our pain to be vulnerably felt and shared with loved ones invites genuine community and generosity. In no way am I encouraging us to be resigned to or victimized by our darkness, and the intention here is not to identify with our depression so that it becomes habitual. However, over time we can discover that suffering has its own natural timing of visiting us, and bring an attitude of acceptance to its unique way of revealing deeper levels of our authenticity. Anyone who has walked through the valley of despair and come out the other side, knows that even in darkness seeds of Light can be found.

It takes courage to be present with darkness when it moves through our own consciousness and those of the people we love. As a living testament to our ability to rise through severe life challenges, Johnny is currently completing his bachelor's degree in mechanical engineering at UC Davis in California, is in a healthy relationship with a woman he loves, and has a purposeful direction in his life.

As part of our family's ongoing crucible with suffering, and in between periods of significant progress, Christian has continued to face significant challenges on his road to recovery. This includes living on the streets as a homeless person, and his tragic struggle with the perils of long-term mental illness and addiction continue to ravage his life.

> *"The most beautiful people we have known are those who have known defeat, known suffering, known struggle, known loss, and have found their way out of the depths. These persons have an appreciation, a sensitivity, and an understanding of life that fills them with compassion, gentleness, and a deep loving concern. Beautiful people do not just happen."*
>
> ~ Elizabeth Kubler-Ross

While most of us excel at distancing ourselves from our pain, each of us is capable of learning to be a sacred witness to all of our experiences. It is a rich way of living to welcome and honor the full range of our experiences, including sadness, anger, fear and depression. Each of us carries the whole spectrum of humanity within us, and life continually provides us with opportunities to consciously meet and embrace it all.

Our deepest unconscious patterns flow from those aspects of ourselves that we are ashamed of. This shame becomes even more potent when we hold something in as our private secret. As we have the strength of heart to divulge our painful secrets to someone with whom we feel safe, sharing our truth brings the liberating Light of compassion to our path.

Life has an uncanny way of ushering us into new and unsettling experiences. Embracing our passages of suffering, however long they last, is a potent avenue for birthing new insights and visions. As we gain the willingness and strength to allow the natural cycles of depression to flow in and through our lives, they will reveal their fertile secrets. Then, lo and behold, we see that darkness can be a powerful and Divine messenger that brings us into a process of rebirth.

"Out of suffering have emerged the strongest souls;
the most massive characters are seared with scars."

~ Kahlil Gibran

Invitation for Discovery

I invite you to reflect upon your life journey and identify a time when you experienced a season of depression. In retrospect, were there any unexpected gifts and insights that this visitation of darkness provided that served your growth? Capture your reflections in your *Journal.*

THE VIEW FROM MY HOSPITAL BED

by Jan Jacobsen

It is midnight.
I am inwardly moaning and complaining about
the moaning, complaining woman next to me
who is keeping me awake.
I want to feel compassion.
And…I want to throttle her.
I ask the nurse, "Is there a quieter room?"
"No."
There is no escape.
How perfect.
I am reading the book, "The Wisdom of No Escape"
about compassion and surrendering to what is.

I surrender.
I cry.
My roomie and I cry together.
I ask about her and she tells me her story.
Her daughter died four months ago, which shattered her heart.
Ten days ago she crashed her car into a tree, which shattered her body.
"I am in so much pain," she says.
I want to hug her.
I want to hold her hand.
How perfect that she is my roommate.
She is reminding me about compassion.
I fall asleep sending her love on my out breaths.
This morning I watched the sun rise
over the mountains.
How wonderful to have this view
from my hospital bed.

SECTION THREE

Embracing Authentic Power & Leadership in Today's World

Through the voyage of your engagement with this book, we have traveled through some fertile territory together. You've discovered that you were born with your relationship with your Authentic Self fully intact. You've begun recognizing some of the ways you may have adapted to life's painful challenges by developing a false self in an attempt to protect yourself.

In turning homeward on your hero's journey, you've embarked on a process of consciously owning the signature qualities of your Authentic Self—and embracing the river of Light in which you belong. Together, we've explored many pathways for cultivating a deeper partnership with both the Divine and human natures within your consciousness, and learned to bring loving compassion to your journey of healing and evolution.

The natural state of human beings is to be fulfilled while living from overflow. In this third section of the book we will dare to move into greater levels of recognizing and sharing our unique gifts, vision and power. By activating our wisdom and brave leadership, we will step forward into new depths of authentic expression that will bless every dimension of our lives.

CHAPTER 12

Opening to Our Authentic Gifts & Calling

"Don't ask yourself what the world needs,
ask yourself what makes you come alive
and then go do it. Because what the world
truly needs is people who have come alive."

~ Howard Thurman

A CHILD'S GIFT

Several years ago I was "garage sailing" one Saturday morning. I came upon a garage sale hosted by a lovely woman and her 6-year-old daughter. The daughter was busy drawing with crayons at a table. The mother mentioned that the girl was selling her drawings. I gently kneeled down at her drawing table and found myself ooohing and aaaahing at her colorful creations. I saw one I liked (it really was charming, of a little girl with a colorful dress), and asked her how much she was selling it for. Her mom said they had agreed upon 25 cents, and the girl looked at me with her big eyes and nodded a yes with a sweet smile. I told her I would like to pay her a dollar for the one I chose, as I really liked it. She looked at me and her eyes grew wide. She was most pleased and joyfully clasped my 4 quarters as I placed them in her delicate hand, and she earnestly said, "Thank you very much!" The mother looked at me with such a sweet look in her eyes (it was that look of gratitude that folks who belong to the "parent club" recognize well). As I was walking away, I overheard the mother whisper to her daughter, "See, I told you honey—you have a gift and people will recognize it!"

EVERYONE IS GIFTED

We are most fulfilled when we dare to share our particular genius with the world. Our Authentic Self knows why we've been incarnated on this planet, and our childlike nature is natively drawn to cultivate and share our gifts with others. When we are supported early on by those around us to create and share the beauty that flows through us, then it is as natural for us to do so as it is for a river to flow.

However, when our attempts to express our gifts are met by others with opposition and discouragement, we may choose instead to protect our Divine treasure by keeping it hidden. Passion, a part of our DNA blueprint, can be rekindled and strengthened. Manifesting this treasure involves transcending our fears and having the courage to live an inspired, open-hearted life. We each have the potential to be a living transmission of Light—rooted in profound trust and deep peace.

IDENTIFYING & CELEBRATING OUR UNIQUE GIFTS

Depth Psychologist and author James Hillman's groundbreaking book, *The Soul's Code*, beautifully captures his acorn theory of human development. In much the same way that a small acorn has the potential to become a vibrant, healthy oak tree, we humans carry a DNA of genius and gifts. The key, of course, is providing the acorn with the right soil, nutrients and conditions.

Just as some seeds in a forest require 2 cycles of frost and thaw, or even a wildfire, to stimulate their germination, so too can growing up in troubling circumstances be precisely what is needed for us to make discoveries about our deeper gifts that we might have missed under seemingly more favorable, less stressful circumstances.

The reality is that everyone is born with a unique constellation of talents. They are inextricably woven into our fabric—yet we may not even know they are there. This is reminiscent of the Buddhist parable of the poor man with a jewel sewn into his coat, of which he is unaware. So the question isn't, "Do I have gifts?" Rather, the core question is, "What gifts am I carrying?"

As the author C.S. Lewis pointed out, "You are never too old to set another goal or dream another dream." With an eye towards trusting the process of discovering and bringing alive your gifts, you may also find reassurance in these words, "That which you're looking for is looking for you."

Your personal power is defined in part by your gifts. As you embrace them and allow their Light to shine through them, you will discover opportunities to make use of them. By simply doing what you are naturally good at and love to do, you make a positive difference in the world around you. To use your talents is to demonstrate to the world that you understand yourself and are attuned to your capabilities.

Many times we overlook opportunities to share our gifts with others. It may be fear of criticism that holds us back or the paralyzing weight of uncertainty. We can all doubt that our innate talents and well-practiced skills could truly add value to other peoples' lives. We feel that our gifts may not be as valuable or worthy of attention as those of others and thus, we hide them away. However, every gift lying dormant and unexpressed within us has the potential to fill a void in our own life and the lives of others.

Meaningful solutions to the overwhelming problems of the world would be closer at hand if it was better understood that each person born bears within them the seed of a gift that the world really needs. Genius is a state of consciousness through which infinite intelligence flows, and life as a whole benefits when we willingly share our gifts.

CARGO

by Greg Kimura

You enter life a ship laden with meaning, purpose and gifts
sent to be delivered to a hungry world.
And as much as the world needs your cargo,
you need to give it away.

Everything depends on this.

But the world forgets its needs,
and you forget your mission,
and the ancestral maps used to guide you
have become faded scrawls on the parchment of dead Pharaohs.
The cargo weighs you heavy the longer it is held
and spoilage becomes a risk.
The ship sputters from port to port and at each you ask:
"Is this the way?"

But the way cannot be found without knowing the cargo,
and the cargo cannot be known without recognizing there is a way,
and it is simply this:
You have gifts.
The world needs your gifts.

You must deliver them.
The world may not know it is starving,
but the hungry know,
and they will find you
when you discover your cargo
and start to give it away.

Invitation for Discovery

What is your *cargo* that you secretly yearn to share with the world? While considering this, it can be beneficial to take time to reflect upon meaningful memories from your childhood and capture them in your *Journal*. Over these years, there may have been things you did not for any specific outcome, but because you found yourself entering into a nourishing, timeless place as you did them. Identifying these fulfilling activities can provide invaluable clues as to your native passions and genius.

EXPRESSING OUR ALIVENESS THROUGH CREATIVITY

As we capture the energy of our unique dream or calling, we open to becoming a focal point for Divine Light to flow through us into this world. This process of flowering as an individual often results in birthing something entirely new into the world—sourced from the higher Presence that ignites the gifts we carry within us. Our Soul is naturally capable of finding its unique expression in the world, and the desire to do so is an impetus for transformation.

The Authentic Self views life as an artist views a canvas. As I define it, an artist is someone who is cooperating with the energies around and within them as they birth something that hasn't existed before.

We are all artists whether we are conscious of it or not, for life is a wondrous creative process that makes humans visible to each other at levels far deeper than our physical appearance and particular occupation. We express ourselves creatively throughout each day with every one of our conscious actions. This may be creating a poem or painting, guiding an organization, scaling a mountain, or taking on the challenge of raising a loving family. We are each creating our own unique life story and, as we do, discovering how we can make a lasting contribution to the world.

Invitation for Discovery

As you look back at the arc of your life, I invite you to identify 2 experiences that stand out as particularly artistic and fulfilling. Although most people don't typically think of themselves as artists, take time to acknowledge those qualities you carry that are artistic in nature, regardless of your profession. Some examples include savoring the process of raising your child in a way that was authentic to you, treasuring the process of cooking, or enjoying becoming more masterful in your business. Capture your notes in your *Journal.*

CREATING FROM GRACE

Once we have a clear vision of what we desire, we can simply give ourselves permission to share this vision with others. Every step we take from that moment on has the potential to lead us in the direction of manifesting this vision.

As you continue in the direction of your heart, you carve for yourself a groove of momentum that becomes easier and easier to follow. Acting on your intentions changes the entire landscape of your life. The secret is momentum, as all your actions taken with heart build up a flow of forward movement that becomes unstoppable.

As you enter into this experience of higher flow, the blossoming of your life can feel predetermined. All you need to do is follow it. Thankfully, the more you get anchored in the momentum of creative energy, the more your mind stops undermining you and your course feels certain. Each step you take towards your vision brings forth new levels of learning and a greater trust in how powerful you are.

MY CALL TO ADVENTURE

One of the most fulfilling experiences in my life was serving for 16 years on Faculty and as the Director of Admissions for the University of Santa Monica. Their progressive 2-year Master's degree program in Spiritual Psychology was an experiential and transformational process. The courses for the program were held one weekend a month for 2 years and attracted students from around the world.

Every year, a new class of students began the 2-year journey. They formed a very close-knit community of up to 250 people per class, who forged deep and lifelong friendships through the course of the program.

I will always be grateful for the bounty I gained through my devoted service to the organization for close to 2 decades on faculty. However, there came a time when I knew in my bones that I was living someone else's vision, and not truly honoring my own deeper life calling and direction.

When my Authentic Self knew it was time to move on, my dreams began revealing to me that I would be leaving the University and moving in a new direction in my life's work. I did not like this emerging truth and wrestled with it for almost a year. I had become quite comfortable in my central leadership role. I was well-paid, was beloved in the community, and was working closely with the directors of the school.

As I struggled with these insistent and intense revelations, I entered into in-depth therapy with a Jungian analyst. I recognized that in unconsciously trying to emulate the directors of the school, over time I had significantly moved away from my authentic expression. In addition, I had given over my spiritual authority to them, mistakenly assuming that they knew better than I did about how I should proceed with my professional life and even with core choices involving my family. I was caught again in the trap of playing out my unconscious false self behaviors which began in my teen years. In my striving to please others to get their approval, I had distanced myself from the wellspring of my own inner wisdom and truth.

I began to see more clearly that I was living a very narrow and safe "spiritual" life. When I was growing up as a teenager, I didn't really have a typical adolescent break from my parents into greater independence. As my consciousness continued to evolve, I began touching into my desire for more freedom of expression and genuine collaboration. My urge for expansive authenticity played itself out by me taking greater risks to share my true perceptions with the directors of the school. This new level of honest, creative expression was not met favorably, and I found it increasingly difficult to breathe my own air on the job.

After months of inner turmoil and healing reconciliation, I explored more honestly the following question: "Am I really fulfilled at my job?" At the time, I had held this question as quite dangerous, as I had been telling myself for years that I would be working at the school for the rest of my life. The way I had set up my relationship with the University resembled a religion, and to ask this question was like entering into forbidden territory. I had avoided it for years. I finally asked it of myself with the courage to hear my deeper truth. I was astonished by the answer I received from my Authentic Self: "No, and in fact you haven't been happy or aligned with being here for quite some time. It is now time for you to embrace your greater gifts and to bring your own inspirational work into the world."

Upon receiving this confirmation of my calling and direction, I resigned from my position and wholeheartedly entered the next great adventure in my life. As it turns out, the wisdom of my Authentic Self, which had been fueling my prophetic dreams, was accurate. Following my departure, I immediately found myself more rested and relaxed and more in touch with my authentic expression. Although I was anxious about how my departure would impact my finances, I had a strong inner sense that, by not giving in to my fears, everything would work out.

Organizations, if engaged at the heart level, can provide an invaluable contribution to the evolution of our Authentic Self. Yet, as with many containers, there often comes a time when the outer structure limits the direct experience of the individual path that each of us has come to express. At these junctures, the call to leave our familiar structure—the known and predictable—is often announced in the wisdom of our dreams and in sensations within our body. When I chose to move on from the University, I needed to summon the courage to leave behind the false sense of security it offered that was no longer aligned with the newly emerging vision for my life.

> *"Great crises and impossible tasks can uncover hidden resources and reveal veins of genius that can alter the course of history. Each soul desires to be part of something greater, something "larger than life," for we each harbor within ourselves a larger life and a greater Self waiting to become known."*
>
> ~ Michael Meade

COURAGEOUS TRANSPARENCY: STEPPING PAST OUR FEARS

In the process of learning to successfully craft our lives in a way that reflects the qualities of our Authentic Self, we must encounter and learn to walk through passages of fear. Though fear is an evolutionary gift meant to sharpen our senses and energize us during times of danger, it can also be a barrier that prevents us from fulfilling our true potential through bold action.

Whether our fear is public speaking, taking part in an activity that makes us anxious, or asserting ourselves with a loved one when we are afraid of how they may respond to us, walking through the fear is challenging. Once we emerge unscathed on the other side, however, we often wonder at how we assumed the worst in the first place. Repeatedly confronting our trepidation head-on helps us accept that few frightening scenarios will ever live up to the disasters that sometimes play out in our minds.

Walking successfully through your fear requires that you turn to the steady presence and sovereignty of your Authentic Self, for this consciousness has the strength to take risks and compassionately support you in holding fear's hand with gentle patience and perseverance. As you do this, a great weight is lifted from your shoulders and you become more fully liberated.

It is challenging to act when you are gripped with fear, so it is wise to start by taking small, easier-to-manage risks. Each time you step past your fear it strengthens you and helps you confront future fears with poise, courage and confidence.

> *"I know these two things for sure: It is not our place to judge the type of goodness we have to offer the world; it is our job to find the courage to offer it. Second, it is our duty to sometimes give beyond what we think we are capable of giving. Despite our inner protestations, that kind of risking and giving expands us, makes us bigger. It clears the way for us to be filled with Love, to be Love."*
>
> ~ Annie O'Shaughnessy

Invitation for Discovery

1. I invite you to identify a time in your life when you were afraid to take a risk—but chose to be courageous anyway. It may have been a time when you were drawn to date someone and asked them despite being afraid they might not like you back. It may have been a professional encounter when you dared to advocate for a promotion or raise. It may have been deciding to jump out of an airplane with only a lightweight parachute on your back.

2. As you reflect upon this experience, take the time to capture in your *Journal* the depth and range of this groundbreaking event. What qualities in you came more alive as you stepped into your daring spirit and crossed this threshold that was once so terrifying? Looking back now, do you have any realizations about how this experience could inspire you to take bold risks in other areas of your life?

LIVING A SHADE BRAVER

Bravery is a cornerstone of the Authentic Self. Bravery is risking to let ourselves be seen as we stand up and become an advocate for ourselves. The hero's journey is about living a courageous life in the face of adversity and emerging triumphant.

Brave action often takes form by having difficult conversations in life. It's telling others about our prayers. It's telling them about our thoughts and feelings that we are tempted to hide. It's acknowledging our vulnerability and asking for support. It's telling someone how much we love them. Magically, our boldness elicits a response from the world around us. It could be as simple as telling your partner that you're hurt. While you may be afraid of being that open, risking consciously is inwardly liberating, independent of the outer result.

"The day came when the risk to remain tight in the bud
was more painful than the risk it took to blossom."

~ Anaïs Nin

Most of us steer away from our Authentic Self, for its nature is to thrive on the presence of truth, which is expansive, and so will always be inviting us to take risks. Having courage involves acting upon what stirs your heart, which invariably brings you face-to-face with your fears. One way to know if you're in touch with what truly matters to you is if you find fear right alongside your excitement. Vulnerability is an excellent indicator that you are genuinely passionate about the new territory you are exploring.

There's nothing wrong with fear, as we all carry this instinctive survival tendency towards anxious imagination and self-protectiveness in the face of something that appears alarming. Fear will always be in the car with you, and the important thing is to not let it grab the steering wheel and drive. You can be in a compassionate relationship with your fears while remaining in charge of your consciousness and actions. Whenever you find that you've given over the reins to fear, which happens to all of us, the key is coming back and allowing your Authentic Self to once again take the lead.

Invitation for Discovery

I invite you to consider an aspect of your life that might be ripe for courageous action. Carefully listen to the whispers of your intuition as you reflect on this invitation. Welcome whatever next steps may be revealed to you from within. Remember, you are not necessarily committing to taking action, rather just allowing yourself to identify a brave risk you could possibly take that would support you in moving forward. Capture any new realizations in your *Journal*.

THE SYNERGY OF FEMININE & MASCULINE ENERGIES

One of the most powerful yet least understood aspects of our Authentic Self involves masculine and feminine energies. When referring to these energies, I am not speaking about gender or sexuality. They are universal human attributes. Both the masculine and feminine are vibrantly available within every individual, regardless of how one identifies with respect to gender. These energies transcend any cultural or societal concepts.

The more we mature and become anchored in our Authentic Self, the more both our masculine and feminine aspects come into full bloom—with an accompanying ability to discern when and how much of each one is needed in any given situation. Nurturing and cultivating our connection with both of these sacred energies deepens our relationship with Divine flow.

"If any human being is to reach full maturity, both the masculine and the feminine sides of the personality must be brought up into consciousness."

~ Mary Esther Harding

Feminine energy is receiving energy. Relative to Spirit, we are all residing in the receptivity of the feminine. It is the source of revelation. When we come into a state of relaxed receptivity to Spirit, which is both our source and essence, we can experience "flow" states. We are receptive to a level of insight and wisdom that informs and sometimes transforms us in ways our logical mind never can.

Our feminine presence carries the seed of love, along with the qualities of compassion, intuition and healing energy. Exhibiting these qualities enhances our capacity to be fully human, and in no way diminishes our masculine energies.

The feminine within us all is also the receiver of inspired visions for our creative expression in the world. It then holds a sacred space in which these visions can take root and grow. The feminine nature inside of us nurtures and supports new possibilities. The natural state of expressing feminine energy is one of grace, of embodying Divine love.

Masculine energy is closely related to manifestation, actualizing a focused vision in the world. This essential aspect of our nature is what allows us to bring into form the mature ideas and visions that the feminine has birthed and nurtured in their infancy. This side of us is more action-oriented and its success is measured more by productivity, real world results, and creative products and services. Protection and empowerment are additional beneficial qualities of the masculine.

Both masculine and feminine energies, however, have shadow sides to them, distortions that come from being out-of-balance. When someone identifies too strongly with their masculine aspect, they can be prone to being impatient, rude, overly competitive and mean-spirited. Until the age of 30, my brother was an extreme example of someone who embodied an imbalanced masculine aspect and was completely shut off from the feminine energies of empathy and compassion, which he later rediscovered and embraced.

If someone over-identifies with their feminine nature, they can be too complacent, find it difficult to stand up for themselves, or have challenges bringing their gifts into the world. As an example of an out-of-balance feminine aspect, my sister's self-destructive addiction to heroin was an extreme form of disempowerment and dependency—like an infant feverishly trying to suckle at a dry breast that was incapable of providing any nourishment—until she connected with her true, internal source of love and strength inside.

BALANCING OUR ENERGIES

The more you are in touch with both the feminine and masculine aspects of yourself, the more you can learn to balance and employ them effectively. Engaging this balance has been the key to my success as a therapist. In my therapeutic work with clients, I often lead with my feminine energies through the qualities of empathy, intuition, healing compassion and nurturing. I engage my masculine energies in service to truthful communication and empowering clients to take charge of the inner and outer dimensions of their lives.

Our masculine and feminine energies are interdependent and designed to be intimate partners within our consciousness. It is possible for all of us to become more fluid and natural in balancing the expression of these energies.

"There is a collective force rising up on the earth today,
an energy of the reborn feminine. This is a time of monumental shift,
from the male dominance of human consciousness back to a balanced
relationship between masculine and feminine."

~ Marianne Williamson

Invitation for Discovery

I invite you to capture in your *Journal* your responses to the following:

1. Which aspects of feminine energy that I've described would you say are your strengths? Which ones might you be well served to strengthen?

2. Which aspects of masculine energy that I've described would you say are your strengths? Which ones might you be well served in strengthening?

3. Identify a time in your life when you felt your masculine nature was predominant in your behavior. What was it like for you?

4. Identify a time in your life when you felt your feminine nature was predominant in your behavior. How was your experience of it?

5. Describe a time in your life when your feminine and masculine energies were both active and flowing through you in a harmonious way.

BLESSED WITH DESIRE

Desire is intimately connected with our sense of Self-worth. The word desire actually comes from the ancient Latin word, desiree, "of the stars." When we are in touch with our genuine desires, our deepest prayers, we are keeping our stars in sight. To embrace our desires is to own our wanting, our longings. When we take this kind of ownership of our lives, the sovereignty of our Authentic Self has full autonomy and we feel worthy of receiving.

Many spiritual paths teach that the root of all suffering is desire. I view the nature of desire from a different perspective. Suffering actually occurs when we either deny our desires or become too attached to them. It's essential to give ourselves full permission to voice and aspire towards our desires, while simultaneously not demanding that life unfold the way we think it should.

Humans are actually blessed with desire. Divine longing flows from deep in your heart, and there's a vibrant presence inside of you that's continually coming more alive. Thus, it's essential to give yourself full permission to breathe life into your desires, for they are intimately connected to the flow of your power and creativity. We often make the mistake of neglecting our desires when we interpret outer conditions to be unfavorable for their fruition. Seen as an opportunity, however, this gap between our current state and our desires can prove fertile soil for activating our resourcefulness, persistence and creativity.

Turning your back on your desires is turning your back on Life. Your challenge and opportunity is to live a life that is, in itself, a work of art. Your life can be a magnificent masterpiece when you dive down, find your beauty, nurture it and offer it to the world.

Invitation for Discovery

I invite you to set aside some generous time by yourself to reflect upon the exploratory questions below, and capture in your *Journal* your responses to 2 or more of them. Bring an attitude of permission, curiosity and innocence to whatever surfaces in your reflections.

1. What would I dare to do if I knew I could not fail?

2. What is it that I uniquely offer the world?

3. Who are my role models, those who stir my heart by how they are living their lives?

4. Who in the world am I jealous of, and which of my specific desires might this feeling be trying to reveal to me?

5. What powerful medicine do I offer others simply through my presence and expression?

SELFISH WITH A CAPITAL "S"

In our culture, selfishness has gotten a bad rap, and most of us grew up constantly receiving messages from our families and others that implied or sounded like, "Well, you certainly don't want to be selfish. Being selfish, that's just not acceptable."

Ultimately, to embrace our deepest desires is not a selfish act. Rather, it is freeing because it opens possibilities for greater exploration, fulfillment and contribution. Embracing our desires is a process steeped in joy and delight, and is ultimately liberating.

If you are to lead a fulfilling life, you must grant yourself permission to be selfish—with a capital S! In this context, there is a distinction between being self-centered and being centered around one's Self. Welcoming Selfishness is a powerful bridge directly to your Authentic Self, the source of your desires. When the depth of your nature is honored and flourishing, you and everyone else around you wins.

JOY, THE COMPASS OF DESIRE

The signature way to recognize something that has deep meaning to you is the presence of joy. A key to connecting with your desires is to identify those things that are absolutely delicious to you. Then, once you've identified them, you can freely invest yourself in exploring and cherishing them.

One of my favorite musicians, Kenny Loggins, tells a story about his 5-year-old son. At one point, Kenny had decided to retire from his singing career, which meant that he would no longer be traveling the world and giving concerts. When he told his son about his decision, the boy became deeply sad. Kenny and his wife could not understand what was troubling him, as one of Kenny's primary motivations for retiring was to spend more time with his family. His son's sadness persisted for several days, until finally the boy burst into tears and said, "If you stop singing, Daddy, you'll die."

Shortly after hearing his son's words, Kenny dove into his next album.

"Life does not require you to sacrifice or
compromise your joy to get what you want.
Joy is what you want,
so when you choose in harmony with it,
you are fulfilling your purpose in living."
~ Alan Cohen

A BLESSED PILGRIMAGE

My private practice began to build steadily. In 2008, I was called to travel with the internationally renowned poet, David Whyte, and 35 others on a 7-day walking tour in Western Ireland. David writes evocative and accessible poetry, and he has been an inspiring mentor to me for well over 30 years.

The days we spent together immersed in the Irish countryside were glorious. We stayed in thatched cottages right on the coast of Galway Bay. Each day we shared poetry, reflected upon our lives, ate wonderful meals, and walked 4 to 5 miles with visits to many ancient Irish landmarks. One day, David's long-time best friend and creative partner, John O'Donohue—a man with vibrant presence and inspiring genius unlike anyone I've ever encountered—spent 3 delicious hours with us one morning.

During the first evening, as we were taking a sunset stroll, I had an intimate conversation with a woman I had just met. She asked, "What is your name?"

I told her I was given the name Norman at birth but had never liked it for myself. I acknowledged that there are some wonderful people who carry that name and it works well for them. However, I felt all my life that it wasn't my true name.

She asked me, "Have you ever considered changing your name?"

I told her I had been secretly wanting to for decades but had convinced myself that changing my name would be vain and superficial.

Her insightful response is etched in my memory: "Really? Why would you want to strap yourself for the rest of your life with a name that you don't resonate with, that's not authentic for you, when you could give yourself the gorgeous gift of a name that you will truly cherish for the rest of your life?"

Her words traveled straight to my heart. She spoke the truth. She spoke my truth. Right then and there, I threw away the name I'd had all my life. In my imagination I saw myself on a boat at sea, joyfully tossing the name Norman, like an old dead fish, overboard. I then committed myself to the adventurous process of discovering a name that I treasured. I let David and the rest of the group know that I had decided to change my name and that I was on a treasure hunt. The whole group supported my plan—and they were excited about it, too! Two days later, another woman on the tour came up to me and said, "You know, you might want to consider a name that was my mother's maiden name, which is Gavin."

As soon as she said the name, its sweet resonance traveled way down inside my body. I immediately said to her, "I love that name. I just love that name."

I came back to the group and shared about what I had been gifted. I told them my new name, beaming. David responded by saying with great gusto, "Wonderful! Well, Gavin it is, then!" It was as if I had been serenaded. It was a coronation.

So, I've been Gavin Frye ever since. I love introducing myself to people using my new name, and I love writing my name. I must tell you, from an Authentic Self perspective, to give myself a name that resonates with who I am has been one of the most sacred gifts I've ever bestowed upon myself. That all this happened while immersed in the healing beauty of the Irish countryside was not a coincidence.

NATURE AS HEALER & TEACHER

When it comes to awakening to our deeper calling, nature is the ultimate medicine. The direct experience of nature leads us beyond our limited selves and reawakens a connection with our hearts.

Indigenous cultures understood that nature is a sacred presence. A profound consciousness permeates the natural world. Yet, unlike more nature-based peoples, modern culture has taught us to forget our connectedness with the natural world. The profound consciousness that permeates the natural world has a deep resonance with our own humanity.

In reality, our Authentic Self and the nature that surrounds us are intimately intertwined and familiar with each other. The ability of plants, animals and landscape to stir us is very real. In nature, we can experience unity and openness to physical, emotional, and spiritual healing. It is our ultimate teacher, healer, and source of comfort.

There is robust scientific data on the beneficial effects of reawakening our connection with the natural world. People who regularly spend time in the outdoors live longer, are healthier, and consistently find greater fulfillment in life. A study on creativity in the wild published in the Public Library of Science found that 4 days of total immersion in nature increased participant creativity as well as performance and problem-solving abilities by over fifty percent. This is consistent with Attention Restoration Theory, which documents that exposure to nature restores our higher cognitive functions.

Another recent study in Stanford, California, compared psychological test results of participants who spent time in nature with those who spent time in urban areas.Those in nature had fewer negative thoughts, were less anxious, and had improved working memory.

The Japanese practice of shinrin-yoku, or forest bathing, which entails wandering in the forest, has calming psychological and physiological effects, including reduced levels of the stress hormone cortisol, lower blood pressure and increased oxygen flow to all cells of the body.

Humans are drawn to and nourished by nature because it only knows how to be authentic—it can't help but be true to its own deeper presence. Thus, when we allow ourselves to be touched by and resonate with nature's energies, they realign us with our own deeper nature.

As human beings, we are desperate to be a part of something larger than ourselves. Yet, unlike nature, humans have the ability to refuse their own growth and blossoming. In the hustle and bustle of our routines, we easily forget the miracle of life that it is to be human and truly alive.

Thankfully, your Authentic Self has the wisdom to recognize its visceral, intimate connection with the natural world. It can remind you of the importance of regularly partaking of nature's freely-given flow of nourishment.

"True ecstasy hails neither from spirit nor
from nature, but from the union of these two."
~ Martin Buber

Invitation for Discovery

1. I invite you to reflect upon and capture in your *Journal* one of your most powerful memories of being moved by the presence of nature. What qualities within you were stirred during this experience?

2. I invite you to take a stroll outside and, as you do, identify an element of nature that calls to your attention. It could be a cloud you see in the sky, some colorful bark you see on a tree, or a bee flying amidst flowers near you—or even an element of nature that may surface within your imagination as you are strolling and witnessing your surroundings.

3. Now, holding your selected nature object in your imagination, give yourself permission to enter into an intimate back-and-forth dialogue with this object. You might, for example, find yourself asking your nature object important questions about an issue or challenge you are currently facing in your life. With an attitude of innocence and curiosity, open yourself to any responses that you imagine may spontaneously come to you from the nature object. This imagined and felt process of dialoguing with nature, entered into with sincerity and openness, can bring surprising and profound new insights. Capture your dialogue and any value you receive from it in your *Journal*.

A NEW CALLING IS BORN

On the last day we were in Ireland, I found myself up well before sunrise. Welcoming the presence of dawn has always been my favorite ritual each day. It was quiet, and I was the only one up. I was sitting in a comfortable chair outside our thatched cottage, overlooking the bay and the smooth hills of Connemara. My heart was so full from the layers upon layers of bounty I'd already received from this magical trip.

That morning, I was left in awe by the arrival of a flow of Divine inspiration. It lasted 30 minutes, during which I was given a vision of creating an 11-month transformational workshop called Sacred Passages. After almost 2 decades of apprenticeship in designing and facilitating transformation, the strong calling revealed to me, from my heart, was to design a workshop that takes place over time and integrates nature with an emphasis on creativity and the sacredness of our bodies.

As I sat there, I simply captured in writing what I was "shown" about all the various elements of this unique offering, including a list of 12 key principles that the work would rest upon. This streaming transmission was given to me and all I had to do was receive it and be blessed by it.

This journey to Ireland was a blessing beyond measure. I was pregnant with possibilities and brimming with new life. I flew home from Ireland to the States, arriving with a new name, a new consciousness, and a blessed vision requesting my care and stewardship.

WHAT TO REMEMBER WHEN WAKING

by David Whyte

In that first
hardly noticed
moment
in which you wake,
coming back
to this life
from the other

more secret,
moveable
and frighteningly

honest
world
where everything
began,
there is a small
opening
into the day
which closes
the moment
you begin
your plans.

What you can plan
is too small
for you to live.
What you can live
wholeheartedly
will make plans
enough
for the vitality
hidden in your sleep.

To be human
is to become visible
while carrying
what is hidden

as a gift to others.

To remember
the other world
in this world
is to live in your
true inheritance.

You are not
a troubled guest
on this earth,
you are not
an accident
amidst other accidents.
You were invited
from another and greater
night
than the one
from which
you have just emerged.

Now, looking through
the slanting light
of the morning
window toward
the mountain
presence
of everything
that can be,

what urgency

calls you to your
one love? What shape
waits in the seed
of you to grow
and spread
its branches
against a future sky?

Invitation for Discovery

I invite you to take a few minutes to contemplate your inner responses to the above poem. Then, leisurely capture in your *Journal* your reflections upon the following questions:

1. What is my true inheritance in this lifetime?
2. What shape waits in the seed of me to grow and spread its branches against my future sky?

CHAPTER 13

Treasuring Our Life As a Sacred River

"...and at the moment of death
you will see the dark roots and the
light roots intertwined and realize that
there is nothing to have changed..."

~ Kahlil Gibran

THE PHENOMENON

As I walked through the grounds of the cemetery, I came over the rise of a hill and encountered a spectacle. A funeral service was taking place. A wooden coffin draped with flowers held everyone's rapt attention. There were easily 400 people surrounding the area of the gravesite, and all of them wore shock and devastation on their faces. The scene took my breath away.

Of the swarm of people surrounding the coffin, at least 100 of them were teenagers experiencing unimaginable grief. As the coffin was lowered into the ground, most of the teens fell to their knees, sobbing and convulsing as they tried one last time to get close to the body and presence of the person that had touched their lives so deeply. That person was my brother, Michael.

He had died one week earlier in a tragic automobile accident—killed instantly when his car inexplicably veered off the road and hit a large tree. As I participated in the funeral service, in addition to feeling my own grief, I was astonished at the depth of mourning by everyone present. After all, he was a former leader of the Aryan Brotherhood and had lived a life of unspeakable violence. How could this spiritual community in a small town in Oregon be experiencing this depth of loss? What had unfolded in Michael's life over these past few years to account for the scene I was witnessing?

Following the burial by his graveside, a memorial service was held for Michael in a large wooden hall that was packed full with the entire church congregation. This celebration of his life lasted well over 4 hours, and it was here that my questions were answered.

I learned that Michael, in the 7 years since he had been released from prison, had become a tower of strength and one of the most respected elders in his church community. Given his own traumatic teen years, he had devoted his loving ministry to mentoring the young adults in the congregation. During the service, dozens of teens described the monumental impact he had on their lives. His courageous transparency regarding all aspects of his past and ultimate transformation is what stirred their hearts so deeply. He knew how easy it was to live life in an arrogant and prejudicial way, and they heeded his caution about judging people based on the color of their skin. His criminal and murderous ways had, in fact, been converted to gold through his demonstrated transformation and in the service of his loving ministry.

As I sat there listening to these testimonials from adults as well as teenagers, my sense of shock slowly alchemized into a sense of wonder. Knowing from my own experience that the depth of one's grief is a measure of the depth of one's love, I realized at that moment how deeply Michael had climbed into the heart of this community. He made an indelible impact upon them. The memorial service moved everyone in attendance in ways that would never be forgotten.

THE ARC & ORCHESTRATION OF AN AUTHENTIC LIFE

Michael was 40 years old when he died—shorty after getting married to his sweetheart, Nancy, who was also an elder in their church. At the time of the accident, he was studying to become a male nurse with a dream of working side-by-side with doctors in the local hospital. He and Nancy were planning on having their first of many children, and his whole life was in front of him.

On the day of my brother's funeral, my waves of sadness were accompanied by waves of revelation. I found myself reflecting upon the entire arc and orchestration of Michael's short yet dramatic life. It dawned on me that there was an intimate relationship between those parts of his life led by his false self and those led by his Authentic Self. The depth of the psychological and spiritual impact he had upon the lives of each teen and adult in his congregation flowed as much from his darker experiences as from his spiritual resurrection.

My deepest intuition revealed to me that Michael had indeed lived a whole and complete life just as it had unfolded, despite his early death. The odyssey was complete. Yes, he was only 40 years old, but what an epic 4 decades he had traversed before his departure. He had come to know his heart and Spirit in profound ways that most people never touch into, and he had generously shared his Light with the world.

I will forever be grateful to my brother for showing me how one person's life can transform hundreds, and even thousands of others when it carries the force of pure love. Michael's life and his death inspired in me a desire to step forward in greater ways to serve others through my own work. It was his final gift to me.

TWO BROTHERS, TWO LIVES

Following the memorial service, I found myself reluctant to leave and began walking the cemetery grounds. Everyone was gone by now. As I neared Michael's burial site, I entered a state of reverie that sparked a flow of memories from his life. I remembered him nonchalantly killing birds with his bb gun as a young teenager; remembered him with his friends spreading guns out on our dining room table as they prepared for a violent encounter; remembered seeing him bound like an animal when we visited him in San Quentin; and then returning for our next visit and witnessing his miraculous transformation expressed in his kindness to the guards; remembered his courageous decision to confess to a cold-blooded murder and accept whatever consequences might come. And I remembered the last time I saw him alive one afternoon in an Oregon hospital as he gently wrapped a cast onto a patient's broken leg. Standing over his grave, I marveled at the way his entire life had unfolded in what seemed to be an orchestrated flow of interconnected experiences.

I then found myself reflecting upon the flow of seminal experiences in my own life. The memories came in a torrent.

I reconnected with myself as an infant feeling the adoration of my father as he arrived home from work in the evening; I remembered looking up at those rare adults whose eyes were filled with Light; I felt again the series of temper tantrums that erupted from the well of loneliness and anguish inside my teenage body. I was back in my college psychology class and

Michael Gardner was weaving his spell, ushering me into my sacred gifts and calling. Once again I was back in the desert with my dad and we were lost until my intuition guided us safely back to our truck. I saw the sea of clients and University students I had been privileged to inspire over many years to touch into their healing and awakening. I felt again the delicious pleasure of Susan arriving in my life, reconnected with the precious memory of reading To Kill a Mocking Bird and other works of classic literature to my young boys as we homeschooled in the trees that surrounded our home; of my marriage coming to a most unexpected and tragic end; and the moment in Western Ireland when the woman suggested to me the name of Gavin.

As I reflected upon these transcendent experiences from my life's journey—the painful and dark ones as well as the joyful and triumphant moments—I realized that each and every experience was essential and had significantly contributed to my growth and evolution. Each event I walked through prepared me for the next, and then the next. Each life lesson that I struggled with, and gleaned well-earned wisdom from, brought me into greater wholeness and assisted me in stepping forward to serve others.

OUR LIFE AS A SACRED RIVER

As I stood there in the quiet of the cemetery, the flow of my own journey and the arc of Michael's life appeared to me as two glorious, winding rivers. An illumination hit me in that moment with a force I will remember forever: each person's life is a sacred river.

As I turned and circled my gaze upon all of the gravesites that surrounded me, I understood that everyone in that cemetery had lived a one-of-a-kind sacred river that carried its own signature. Our rivers flow independently but are also profoundly interconnected. Each member of my brother's congregation had a unique sacred river that had intimately interwoven itself with Michael's river.

At that moment, I reconnected with the incandescent dream from earlier in my life—the one in which I was shown a shimmering, golden river of Light available to everyone. I had known about the sacred river all along on some level, but now I knew it consciously. As this new understanding flooded my awareness, I felt nobility in my heart towards humanity and the sacredness of life. I wept with gratitude.

ILLUMINATING OUR SACRED RIVER

Each of us has a unique life journey, and the authentic stories from our lives carry depth and meaning that often elude us at the time they occur. It is usually in retrospect that we are able to recognize the greater impact and significance of our experiences.

My brother Michael's story exemplifies this phenomenon. Who could possibly have imagined that his life's immersion in violence and hatred would lead to an awakening that would put him in the perfect position to inspire hundreds and change the course of so many young lives for the better?

By sharing my personal life stories in an intimate way, my hope is to encourage you, the reader, to treasure your own life's mysterious unfolding. As was revealed to me, when we link the seminal moments of our lives into the arc of fulfilling the deeper path of our Authentic Self—we recognize the uniquely orchestrated signature of our sacred river. This process of consciously embracing our multi-faceted life journey gives us direct access to authentic power.

The 19th-century philosopher, Arthur Schopenhauer, points out that when you reach an advanced age and look back over your lifetime, it seems to have had a consistent order and plan, as though chronicled by a novelist. Events that, when they occurred, had seemed accidental or of little significance, turn out to have been indispensable elements of a coherent plot. So who hatched that plot?

Schopenhauer suggests that, just as your dreams are orchestrated by an aspect of yourself of which your conscious mind is usually unaware, so too is your whole life designed by a deeper presence and intuition within you. As people whom you met by mere chance became leading agents in your life, similarly you have served—often unknowingly—as an agent in the lives of others. Ultimately, the many threads of our life story interweave with the threads of other people's stories and events into a grand tapestry that reveals the big picture of the journey we've been on all along.

In my transformational workshops, I invite participants to identify the most moving life experiences they've had. As they step back and review these consequential events, their unique sacred river illuminates itself, revealing its previously hidden secrets, treasures and patterns. This in-depth exercise, which I outline below, provides you with fertile access to the storehouse of wisdom within the Authentic Self.

Invitation for Discovery

Consider setting aside a few hours for the purpose of reviewing your entire life as a sacred river. You may be drawn to complete this process in several stages.

One at a time, identify 10 to 15 of the most unforgettable, impactful experiences from your life journey. Whether they be positive and uplifting or painful and challenging, the main criteria for selecting these core experiences is that they stirred the very depth of your being. They were the moments when you were the most fully present.

It doesn't matter whether the rest of the world would consider these moments relevant or important. In fact, they could be remarkably simple. What's essential is your perspective and interpretation of each experience, and the pivotal role it played in your life. These are the seminal experiences that, for whatever reason, have stayed with you, marked you, changed you.

As you identify each of them, give yourself the gift of adequate time to reconnect with the experience and capture in writing your memories and reflections. If it was an uplifting memory, can you reunite with the glorious experience of being deeply moved? If it was a painful memory, can you reconnect with the pain of what happened?

After you have identified these milestones in your life, you can consciously string them together in the order in which they occurred. As you do so, this review process can evolve organically such that you will actually begin perceiving the DNA strands of your life, the unique fingerprint of an unfolding existence that is yours alone.

You may glimpse patterns. Core lessons repeated throughout your life will often reveal themselves. The process is akin to being in a movie theater, watching a movie of your life unfolding on the screen. Writing down the most essential experiences of your life is also much like creating a screenplay about yourself. It allows for an insightful witnessing of your life. As well, the process of illuminating your unique sacred river is an opportunity to bring healing compassion to any passages that still carry a measure of pain or judgment.

You also may find yourself recognizing and treasuring your own genius, beauty, and the unique ways you've made contributions to the lives of others. No two people are alike and we each feel pain in our own way, heal in our own way, and love in our own way. This isn't about promoting an ego stance of, "I'm the most special." The reality is we're all equally miraculous and one-of-a-kind. Furthermore, the more you treasure your own sacred river, the greater appreciation you'll have for the sacred rivers of others.

Once you have identified and laced together your key life experiences, place your notes together somewhere in your home where you can re-visit and touch into them. Let them breathe and reveal themselves to you over time in a spacious way. This is a process of contemplation, of allowing your relationship with all of your potent experiences to steep within you just as you would with a fine tea. The intelligence of the heart makes the invisible visible.

As a final step in this process, it can be quite moving and richly anchoring to choose someone in your life, someone you honor and trust, with whom to share your sacred river. This can be done verbally, or perhaps as a dance, or a poem, or even by creating a painting or visual representation of your river. However you are guided to share the deeper currents of your life, doing so can provide a rich opportunity for taking in, on another level, the precious gift of your one-of-a-kind flow of experiences.

You may also find yourself returning to visit your sacred river from time to time over the years and discover subtle yet profound new insights about the unique way your life has unfolded.

Your sacred river continues to unfold and to reveal itself throughout your lifetime. New seminal experiences will find you and have their imprinting ways upon you. Maintaining an intimate connection with this deeper flow is a wise investment.

"Our deepest fear is not that we are inadequate.
Our deepest fear is that we are powerful beyond measure.
It is our Light, not our darkness, that most frightens us.
We ask ourselves, 'Who am I to be brilliant, gorgeous,
talented, fabulous?' Actually, who are you not to be?
You are a child of God. Your playing small does not serve
the world. There is nothing enlightened about shrinking
so that other people won't feel insecure around you.
We are all meant to shine, as children do. We were
born to make manifest the glory of God that is within us.
It's not just in some of us; it's in everyone. And as we
let our own light shine, we unconsciously give other
people permission to do the same. As we are liberated
from our own fear, our presence automatically liberates others."

~ Marianne Williamson

CHAPTER 14

Embodying Authentic Power & Leadership

"The most powerful force on earth is the human soul on fire."

~ Ferdinand Foch

WELCOMING AUTHENTIC POWER

Being in a flow with Divine energy is the way to access authentic power. As we anchor a connection with the presence of our deeper nature, our power increases exponentially.

It is when we contract in response to stress, and then try to dictate how we think things should be, that we fall out of our conscious connection with this flow of sacred energy. Though it may sound counterintuitive, we regain our connection by giving up the illusion of control and letting life decide how it will unfold.

As we cooperate with this organic flow, we stop wasting energy on self-defense and in trying to make things conform to our will. We reclaim vital energies and strengthen our connection with a natural and abundant source of power.

This is exactly how your physical body works. You don't have to consciously make up your mind about the thousands of ways your body is continuously functioning and taking care of itself. Without you telling it what to do, you have a relationship of faith with your body as it carries on its countless miraculous operations every moment.

"Our goal is to move from the external power of the personality into the authentic power of the Soul. Access to the Soul is continually available. How much you avail yourself of it is up to you."

~ John-Roger

Invitation for Discovery

I invite you to reflect upon your life and identify a time when you experienced being infused with love or joy, for no particular reason, and found yourself acting with relaxed, natural confidence. What was meaningful to you about this experience? What were the outcomes of those actions, and how did they influence those around you at the time? Capture in your *Journal* your reflections surrounding this experience.

FALSE POWER

People are perpetually surprised that those who rise to power tend to abuse it rather than use it in ways that enhance justice and serve the greater good. Yet, inevitably, if someone is wielding political power from a place that is not rooted in the nobility and security of the Authentic Self, their sense of false power will overtake them like an addictive opiate. It is this false relationship to power that leads them to commit egregious abuses of authority in order to get their daily "fix" and retain control.

Most people who gain political power have not done the work of inner transformation in the realm of compassion, and millions of people suffer as a consequence of their unconsciousness. This is why many come to the conclusion that all power is corrosive to the character of those who possess it.

Yet, the root of the word authority is the same as that of author and authentic. It's important to recognize that there are powerful and healthy forms of genuine authority available to us that are characterized by love and respect. Imagine a whole government comprised of people committed to acting from their highest integrity with the intention of supporting the greatest good of all. This is the caliber of leadership that honors and celebrates the wisdom that resides within us all.

CREATING WITH SPIRIT AS MY PARTNER

Upon returning home from my brother's funeral, I had an inner experience of being asked by Spirit to begin taking specific steps to design and facilitate an 11-month transformational program, Sacred Passages. The initial burst of inspiration for this work came to me in Western Ireland. What was radical about this experience was that it involved a conscious conversation with a Presence larger than me. I had never before experienced an internal, back-and-forth dialogue of this kind that was irrefutably not all in my head.

"You're asking me to step forward and make this program happen?" I asked Spirit.

And Spirit responded," Yes."

With sincere curiosity, I asked, "Why me?"

The Spirit of Life said, "Well, it's easy to explain. You see, we don't have hands. We can't make phone calls. We can't make copies and handouts. We can't collect money. We don't have a voice to facilitate the program. You are capable and have been well trained. We've selected you for a particular reason. You've been mentoring in the process of designing and facilitating this depth of work for 20 years. We're aware of who you are. We would like to have you as our partner. Would you be willing to consider that?"

I found myself responding, without hesitation," Yes."

There was a benevolence, a humility, a power with this Presence—and yet our conversation had a matter-of-fact quality about it. The Presence was strong and soft at the same time.

And then I asked, "Well, how will this work; how will we work together?"

The Presence replied, "If it is OK with you, we'll take the lead. All you have to do is follow. We'll help you come up with the themes and processes. We'll direct you with everything you need to do from the time we start this initiative until it comes to completion."

And I responded, "Oh, I like that, I really like that, because I'm a little nervous about this."

Spirit replied, "We understand. We'll be specific and help you each step of the way. You will receive creative inspiration throughout the process of designing the marketing materials, filling the program through outreach and sales, as well as designing and facilitating the workshop for each of the 11 months. We will be right there with you—in the lead."

This intimate conversation with Spirit moved me, calmed me, and filled me with trust for its word. Indeed, in the months ahead, Spirit followed through with everything it said it would do and more. Through a regular back-and-forth dialogue, I was given a grounded series of inspired ideas that I implemented with great ease. Spirit provided all of the key elements and overall direction, including facilitating the discovery of the exquisite site in nature where I chose to hold the event.

About 2 months before the program launched, fear crept in. I found myself procrastinating in taking the next steps required. I realized that I had begun asking myself, "Will the workshop be successful?" Each time, the answer from my mind was a resounding, "No," which only increased my anxiety.

During meditation one day, I asked Spirit to reveal to me a more fundamental, constructive question I could be asking myself. The new question I was provided with was, "Am I willing to put my whole heart into the program?" My answer to this question was an immediate, "Yes!" The authority of Divine inspiration, coupled with the years of inner work I had done, enabled me to break through the barrier of fear. I then moved right back into the flow of preparations for the program.

Throughout the entire series, there was a dynamic partnership with this invisible Presence that was grounding, calming and real. The 11-month program was remarkably successful. We held it in a breathtaking location in nature and included an emphasis on creativity and embracing the sacredness of our bodies. Each of the 16 participants within the intimate community had major life transformations—including healing from a range of deep inner traumas, the triumphant writing and publishing of inspirational books, successful career transitions and the launch of new businesses. They each had the opportunity to embrace, share and interweave their sacred rivers. Most of them are close friends with each other to this day. It was one of the most meaningful experiences of my life.

AUTHENTIC LEADERSHIP

True leadership emanates from a deeply spiritual consciousness. It is a process of learning to turn towards Spirit, towards our Authentic Self inside, and say, "Please use me more fully," and then learning to follow its lead. Surrendering to our highest Self, we are capable of following this natural flow of guided direction. This kind of intimate relationship with Spirit is available to everyone without exception.

I am reminded of the story of an indigenous tribe that has lived in the South Pacific for thousands of years. This tribe regularly canoes hundreds of miles from one island to another. To navigate, their tradition is for the elder in the tribe to lie down with his soft, bare belly pressing against the inside bottom of the canoe. With no physical landmarks to guide them, the elders would enter into this intimate communion with the ocean to access their inner compass in order to successfully navigate the sea.

This story captures an ancient, highly effective ritual in which people were trained to rely upon an empathic rapport with the elements of nature as their navigation system—long before mechanical sea-faring instruments were created. It was a form of sacred leadership that required no words. Yet, it reminds us of the challenge we are each faced with every day as we learn to navigate an awake, unrehearsed existence by being in direct contact with the elements of life.

Living our lives intuitively does not mean we will not stumble. What it does mean is that we will learn from each of our experiences, which allows us to gain a greater ability for making aligned choices. The more we listen in this deeper way, the more we become aware of the subtleties of these Divine messages and can rely upon their enduring and elevated nature.

Invitation for Discovery

1. Was there a time in your life when your intuition, your inner compass, provided you with specific direction and counsel regarding a project you were working on? What form did it take (e.g. a voice, a dream, an intuitive sense or feeling, etc.)? What

was the guidance you received? How might you make yourself more available to listen to and honor this source of wisdom in an ongoing way? Capture your reflections in your *Journal*.

2. If you were to have an internal conversation with the larger Spirit of Life as you know it, what aspect of your life would you like it to be about? Once you identify this area of inquiry, take a few relaxed, deep breaths. Next, engaging your imagination, I invite you to enter into an intimate dialogue with Spirit about this area of your life. When you are complete, record any insights you receive in your *Journal*.

THE VULNERABLE UNKNOWN

Once I recognized the truth that I was to move on from my marriage with Susan, my life was catapulted into vulnerability. Major change was now unfolding in 2 central dimensions: after almost 3 decades, I was ending a committed relationship while also facing the question of where I would choose to call my new home. As sure as I was about my direction, I was frightened as I entered this new frontier.

Following the traumas we had faced as a family, we were in significant debt. The waves of grief over the demise of our marriage were excruciating, and I was faced with picking up the pieces of my life and beginning anew. In addition, of course, I continued to be as emotionally and financially supportive as possible of Susan and our sons.

For the first time in 30 years, I was completely on my own. It was overwhelming. Thankfully, having reconnected with my deeper truth, despite the overwhelm I was more anchored in the knowing and resiliency of my Authentic Self. It rose to the occasion.

I treated every step involved in the process of ending our marriage as a sacred act. I was tender with myself and Susan through our grief. I walked through an interminable passage of legal and financial steps, including selling our home. Throughout, I was reckoning with the shock that I had—seemingly out of nowhere—joined the ranks of men and women who have experienced divorce.

One day during this time, I had an epiphany. I remembered I'd been holding a neglected prayer in my heart for decades: a secret desire to live in the Pacific Northwest. I had spent my entire life in the bright sun and dry landscape of Southern California. Being a fair-

skinned man with an Irish lineage, I longed for lush green and rainy countryside. Honoring this instinct, I embarked on a 2-week road trip to the Pacific Northwest. Much like the indigenous elders who navigated their canoes through Polynesian waters, I listened closely to where my inner knowing was guiding me to live. As soon as I arrived in Portland, Oregon, I fell in love with the city. While I wasn't prepared to make a final decision, I drove back home to Southern California with a renewed sense of purpose, revitalized by the life energies of the forests I had journeyed through.

A few things had to be figured out before making the move, the most important of which involved my work. Could I continue to do my work in Portland? I realized that the answer was yes, as at that point I was already mentoring almost all of my clients on-line via video conferencing. At that moment, my draw to make Portland my new home propelled me forward.

After finding a place to lease through a website, I loaded up my car and a U-Haul trailer with all my belongings. I drove 16 hours straight to Portland, arriving at my new home at one in the morning. It was pitch black outside, and I was exhausted. The moment I entered, I recognized that I had made a catastrophic blunder. The photos on the internet were misleading; it was too dark and claustrophobic. I knew I would be miserable there.

My car and U-Haul were in the driveway. I had already paid first and last month's rent, most of which would be non-refundable as this was my error. I had nowhere to go, and I was fatigued after driving all day and night. I cried and cried.

As I got back in the car and drove away, it started to snow. I adore snow, and at that point in my life, I'd had only a handful of experiences of being in freshly fallen snow. Then it began to snow heavily. In that moment, with nowhere to go and everything in the world I possessed packed in the trailer behind me, I found myself entranced by the beauty surrounding me. In my marrow, I sensed the snowfall was an auspicious sign of what was to come. I had an abiding faith that indeed all was going to work out. I felt blessed as I was surrounded by the unknown, the gloriously snow-blanketed unknown...

NEW ROOTS

After driving through the snow for awhile, still scared but now wide open with anticipation and wonder, I pulled off the road and slept for a few hours in my car. When I awoke, the car was blanketed with snow. I drove to a 24-hour diner and bought myself a glorious vegetable omelette breakfast—with a chocolate shake!

It was a Sunday morning and I scanned the Craigslist rental ads. My very first call was to the man who would become my new landlord. The place was available for me to view within an hour, and as soon as I saw it, I knew it was perfect. My new abode was the ground-floor granny flat in his beautiful home.

This new space, where I would begin to carve out my new life, was only 425 total square feet, including a small kitchen. Yet, after 25 years of marriage, of intensely cohabitating with others amidst all the gut-wrenching trials of Susan and me raising and serving our 2 sons, to me this new home was huge.

SYNCHRONICITY

One of the great gifts of authentic power is synchronicity. An example of synchronicity, sometimes referred to as serendipity, is the experience of walking down the street and stumbling into a stranger who you end up marrying a year later. These are unplanned and wildly unexpected occurrences in the flow of our lives. And yet, moving through life with a conscious orientation towards the heart seems to invite such occurrences with a high degree of regularity.

I know a woman who created a multi-million dollar business by teaching people how to paint with watercolors. She is remarkably gifted. When I asked her how she discovered this talent, she told me a wonderful story. She and her husband were moving from Chicago to Los Angeles. When the moving truck with all her belongings arrived, there was one box in it that did not belong to her. It happened to be filled with all the supplies someone would need to do watercolor painting, something she had never done in her life. She made repeated attempts with the moving company to identify the original owner of the box, all in vain. They encouraged her to simply keep it, and she ended up storing the box in her garage. A few months later, while struggling with depression, she suddenly became curious about painting with watercolors. She went into the garage, found the box, and opened it. Lo and behold, watercoloring became her therapy. Surprisingly, she discovered she had a natural gift for it. Within a couple of years, she launched her own business teaching the art and craft of watercolor painting.

The reality is that we often don't know how and when our calling will emerge into the world of form, and that's the mystery and beauty of it.

AN UNEXPECTED COMMENCEMENT

Once I finally had my own space and privacy, a pervasive stillness swept over me. I had entered into a sacred passage that was about nourishing my roots. Over the first few weeks of furnishing my new home, I had synchronistic encounters with beautiful objects at second hand stores from all around Portland. I followed my intuition in choosing each one, steadily making my home a loving sanctuary. The pleasure of creating my own living space in ways that honored my aesthetic tastes, without having to consider the preferences of anyone else, was exhilarating. After so many years of tending to my now-adult children, a neglected part of myself experienced deep nourishment from this kind of tending.

I received confirmation that my Authentic Self, in this body, in this life, simply loves green trees and the rain and rivers. It also loves the cold and fires and warm sweaters. I was discovering firsthand that the physical landscape of where one lives is a critical aspect of being aligned with one's Authentic Self.

With each passing week, I recognized that something profound was happening within me. A new consciousness was emerging from deep inside of me. All the years of pain and suffering I'd endured with our family had, unbeknownst to me, ushered me into new levels of freedom, strength and wisdom. I hadn't realized until now the transformation that had been occurring under the surface during this long trial by fire.

I also discovered new kinds of music that opened up new spaces within me. I purchased a 12-foot solo canoe that only weighed 33 pounds, and spent time in the early morning hours gently paddling on the pristine alpine lakes outside of Portland. I would just drift and be one with the water while mountains of green trees surrounded me in the mist, as time disappeared. Quite often, there was no one on the lake but me. Being in this luscious landscape brought me alive.

I spent 18 months all to myself in my new home. I didn't date, and I didn't want to. I was hibernating in healing and deepening mode, opening up to receive in greater ways than ever before. This extended time of loving courtship with my Self was the richest year of my life.

Although I had very few dollars in my bank account, that granny flat was a palace and I felt like a prince. During the unforgettable months I lived there, I never felt wealthier in all my life. The calling I had carried for over a decade to step forward to write this very book now grew stronger and more joyfully insistent. I had the sense that I was being prepared for a new level of self-expression. I felt pregnant, as if something was gestating inside me that was to be birthed—something that might make a real difference in people's lives. I couldn't wait to see what Spirit was bringing my way...

INNER LEADERSHIP FLOWS INTO OUTER LEADERSHIP

As opposed to power imposed through force, heart-centered power through inspiration is the true nature of authentic leadership. Self-knowledge gained through the maturing of consciousness is the source of truly effective, wise leadership that transforms lives.

The most challenging person we will ever learn to lead is ourselves, which is why cultivating the ability to access our inner guidance is so essential. Because we are all interconnected, our effective Self-leadership naturally overflows into authentic leadership in all our relationships.

The mark of a true leader is one whose main interest is empower-ing others to lead themselves rather than seducing them to being bound to external leadership. False leaders often encourage us to depend upon them as our source of strength.

There is nothing wrong with looking to another with respect and reverence and learning from them. It is an essential part of the human journey. The key, however, is to find a person who truly sees and honors us and seeks to empower us to be our own authority. Real leaders are consummate listeners and healers. They bring their compassion to our suffering, which enables us to embrace and transcend our fears and limitations.

The prevailing paradigm of most modern political and corporate leaders is still to force their way to the top by spinning the truth, manipulating constituencies and buying their way into power. These imposter leaders cannot command true respect or loyalty because their expression is led by a hunger for power rather than a desire to sincerely serve others. Only leaders who cannot be corrupted have true authority at their disposal. These are the individuals who are guided by their own inner Light—and not by their addictive need for validation from others and authority over them.

True leadership is sourced upon an ideal of service. To effectively lead a person or group of people, we need to put aside our own opinions and judgments, listen intently to the needs being expressed, and honor Spirit's promptings within us.

People who carry the gift of leadership have a magnetic presence, and just by being around them we can come to new insights and clarity about our own direction. These people often have an uncanny way of helping others to see underlying patterns and attune to the greater good. Given their steady connection with an expanded level of intelligence, their guidance tends to be in alignment with the way the future is naturally unfolding.

Authentic leadership is in harmony with higher virtues. This does not mean grandiose—indeed, the power of small, unseen virtuous acts in relationships is incalculable. My dad's mechanic friend, Johnny Wilkes, spent 10 minutes gently assisting me with my motorcycle at a time of trauma when I was 13, and his kind actions forever changed my life. Genuine facilitators of people and consciousness make communications and implementation smoother. Although they are supremely capable of leading from the front, they are skilled at fostering a space in which an organic team harmony can develop on its own with minimal interference. If needed, they are content to encourage others with the requisite gifts to stand forward and rise to meet challenges while they themselves support quietly from behind the scenes.

This is the true meaning of guidance—trusting in the life process, rather than forcing matters by taking control. Virtue lies beyond the need for recognition, with the source of true leadership being an ability to collaboratively surrender to the flow of life itself.

Ultimately, all arenas of leadership need to evolve until they shift from embodying fear to love, and from self-serving to whole-serving. For us to step into authentic leadership, we must first recognize the power within ourselves. As we do this, a tide of intelligence and optimism flows through us out into the world. Transcendent leadership is about recognizing that there is loving greatness in everyone.

"If your actions inspire others to dream more, learn more, do more and become more, you are a leader."
~John Quincy Adams

Invitation for Discovery

1. In what areas of your life are you experiencing yourself as an effective leader? This could involve any personal or professional areas of expression, including caretaking animals you love, serving your children or your parents when they are in need, or being supportive to a friend or co-worker as they are going through a time of challenge.

2. Do you have any intuitions about specific areas of your life where you might cultivate the next level of your authentic leadership? What specific steps might you take to manifest this level of expansion? Capture notes in your *Journal*.

TRIUMPH & ABUNDANCE

Around this time, my professional work took a most unexpected turn. It began when an entrepreneurial couple came to me for relationship therapy. They loved each other a great deal, but were buckling under the pressures of leading their respective businesses. Conflicts had mounted in their relationship, as they did not have safe, effective communication skills in place to resolve their differences.

My work with them allowed their relationship to flourish, and simultaneously resulted in leaps in the level of empowered leadership they brought to their respective businesses. I'd worked with entrepreneurs in the past, but my work with this couple was different. I accessed new levels of clear perception and witnessed myself bringing forward new gifts that served both their personal and professional transformations in exponential ways.

Grateful to receive this life-changing work, the couple referred me to a stream of other entrepreneurial couples. Like themselves, these couples were highly successful in the business realm, yet were thirsty for psychological and spiritual growth—individually and within their relationship. In addition to manifesting outer success and the wealth that accompanied it, they had a sincere desire to experience deeper meaning and fulfillment.

My practice soon became almost entirely dedicated to serving as a spiritual therapist and leadership mentor to entrepreneurs from around the world. For the first time, I had to create a waiting list for new clients. I remember one morning, the week after I had mustered the courage to raise my rates, being astounded as yet another large deposit had arrived in my bank account. Each time I looked at my burgeoning bank balance—and I'm embarrassed to admit this—I became giddy like a little kid.

During this period of robust expansion, I realized that my dream of purchasing a beautiful waterfront home somewhere in the Pacific Northwest, as well as my long-held prayer of writing a book about my life and work, were quickly coming into view on the horizon. All the inner and outer work I had done for decades was coming to fruition.

FUTURE SELF-DIALOGUE

Dawna Markalova's poem and book of the same name, *I Will Not Die an Unlived Life*, serves up an interesting invitation. It asks, "When we are on our death bed, what kind of life will we look back on?" In essence, will we or will we not have significant regrets about the choices we've made at crucial points in our lives? How much triumph and sweet fulfillment have we denied or welcomed onto the stage of our life?

Whenever you are faced with a significant life decision, encountering a fork in the road that gives you pause, you can employ the powerful technique of Future Self Dialogue. At these times, you can enter your active imagination, travel to a time in the future when you are approaching the end of your life, and consult with the wise elder within you. This presence can provide invaluable guidance regarding the challenge you are currently facing.

This more mature and seasoned consciousness has an enhanced perspective. When you access this future self, you can actually attune to and taste what it feels like to reside in the experience of two very different possible futures that may unfold. You can also ask this future self, "Which choice is the most courageous, the most aligned with my heart?" As you remain open, relaxed and trusting, you may receive clear inner guidance about your way forward, which is often accompanied by a distinct presence of peace and knowing. In times like these, you are actually not making a decision. You are simply attuning to a clear inner directive.

It's empowering to step away from the current reality of your life, where you're locked into your present circumstances, into an expanded, macro-perspective. This is a dynamic tool that uses the fulcrum of age to access your deeper wisdom for how to live your life more boldly and authentically.

Invitation for Discovery

1. I invite you to identify a significant life choice that may be looming on the horizon. Take some time to connect with your future self about this life choice. Bring to this elder version of yourself your specific challenge or creative opportunity. Take the time you need to share the full range of your current experience, including your enthusiasms, anxieties, callings, hesitations, etc.

2. Once you have given full voice to all the inner voices that are present, give yourself permission to dialogue with your future self, including asking any specific questions you may have. As you do, avail yourself of the wisdom that flows from this more experienced and evolved version of yourself. Capture your experience of this dialogue in your *Journal*.

BECOMING A SPIRITUAL WARRIOR

Given that we live in a fierce world, being on a path of leadership often asks us to face and grow from life's challenges. As you stand forward to share your Light, to express your gifts and calling, people and circumstances may oppose you. Our world is often designed to test you and to help you become more anchored in your strength. When this takes place, you may experience life as a battleground. Perhaps someone you work with is saying negative things about you. Rather than retaliating in a destructive way, you might call upon what I refer to as your spiritual warrior, who is actually highly capable of reckoning with such challenges by responding with transformative love, wisdom and patience.

At times like these, we can ask ourselves, "What are the spiritual qualities I can bring to bear as I'm facing this challenge?" A powerful example of a spiritual warrior would be Nelson Mandela. As punishment for his resistance to racism in South Africa, he spent 27 years of his life behind bars. While in prison, he furthered his education, wrote letters, continually made a difference in the lives of his fellow inmates—and wisely prepared himself to serve the greater good. He envisioned the kind of person he would have to be in order to begin leading his country beyond its violent racial divide. As a testament to his determination, he actually began helping his country steer itself out of apartheid even before he was released from prison.

Once he was released, he soon stepped into the majesty of serving his nation as President, overcoming seemingly insurmountable odds as he worked towards uniting South Africa's diverse population politically, economically, emotionally and spiritually. He gave everything he had. The blessing of his presence and actions impacted every one he encountered. He was a profound demonstration that the Authentic Self, in its most dynamic form, operates from inspiration and has a vast potential to shape humanity.

> *"No one is born hating another person because of the color of his skin, or his background, or his religion. People must learn to hate, and if they can learn to hate, they can be taught to love, for love comes more naturally to the human heart than its opposite."*
>
> ~ Nelson Mandela

A PERSONAL & POLITICAL TRANSFORMATION

Vaclav Havel was a Czech statesman, writer and former dissident. He is a supreme example of someone who was catalyzed from the pain and darkness of his inner life into an expression of groundbreaking political power that contributed to the collapse of communism in Czechoslovakia in 1989.

Vaclav lived a life of resistance—and resilience. As a young man in post-World War II Prague, his hopes of studying the humanities in college were dashed, and his family's wealth was stolen by the communists who had seized Czechoslovakia. At one point, Vaclav entered an extended season of suffering, deeply depressed and teetering on the edge of ending his life. He realized he was immersed in a divided life: on the outside living in conformity to the rules of the communist regime, and on the inside carrying a yearning for freedom, truth and justice.

A gifted poet and playwright, Havel's controversial writings highlighted the moral bankruptcy of the imperialist system. By 1968, the year the Soviets invaded Prague, Havel's writing had already won him international acclaim. It also increasingly made him a target of the state. His works were banned in his country and he was forbidden to leave Czechoslovakia. As a political dissident, Havel braved the surveillance, threats and violence that those who speak out against tyranny often endure. He launched several dissident organizations and spent 4 years in prison.

In 1975, at the risk of being killed or thrown into prison again, Havel wrote an open letter to Gustav Husák, who was then the general secretary of the Communist Party of Czechoslovakia. It warned of the dangerous consequences of the repression of normal social life and the humiliation of human dignity.

With this letter, he was essentially going public with the fact that he was not going to take it anymore and suggested he was not the only one who felt this way. He wrote that the communist regime was inhumane and cruel, and he was no longer going to betray himself or his people by collaborating, even through his silence, in the evil that had overcome the culture and society he loved. Vaclav was placed under house arrest, but his letter circulated as the underground bible of small activist groups who found in it a confirmation of their own story, a story of the wounded heart.

As communism teetered in 1989, due to his courageous voice he became a leading player and chief negotiator in the Velvet Revolution, the Prague street protests that destroyed totalitarianism in Czechoslovakia. The New York Times called the revolt "so smooth that it took just 2 weeks to complete, without a single shot fired."

Havel went on to become the democratically elected President of Czechoslovakia and the Czech Republic from 1989 to 2003, just months after languishing in a prison cell. It was an unlikely role, since he was unassuming and something of an introvert. He was also unfailingly polite and possessed a humility most world leaders lack. His reserve ultimately made him a better leader, as he held space for the dissolution of years of communist oppression. Vaclav actively supported like-minded dissidents around the world, and in his lifetime was awarded just about every international human rights award.

Havel was asked in later years if he wrote that open letter to initiate the movement that brought communism down in Czechoslovakia. He said, "No, I wrote that letter as a matter of auto-therapy to keep from committing suicide." He said he had come to a place where he had to either express the truth of his heart in an outer way in the midst of a very cruel and oppressive political system, or take himself out. There was no longer a choice.

HANDS

by Jewel

If I could tell the world just one thing
It would be that we're all ok
And not to worry because worry is wasteful
And useless in times like these
I will not be made useless

I won't be idled with despair
I will gather myself around my faith
For light does the darkness most fear
My hands are small, I know,
But they're not yours they are my own
But they're not yours they are my own
And I am never broken

Poverty stole your golden shoes
But it didn't steal your laughter
And heartache came to visit me
But I knew it wasn't ever after

We will fight, not out of spite
For someone must stand up for what's right
Cause where there's a man who has no voice
There ours shall go singing

In the end only kindness matters
I will get down on my knees and I will pray

My hands are small, I know,
But they're not yours they are my own
And I am never broken
We are never broken.
We are God's eyes God's hands God's mind.
We are God's eyes God's hands God's heart.

CHAPTER 15

An Awakened Civilization

"The greatest gift you can give is that of your own Self-transformation."

~ Lao Tsu

Let me congratulate you for completing the in-depth journey of healing and awakening that accompanies the reading of this book. You've initiated a profound process of change and growth by becoming more connected with the real you, your Authentic Self. Thank you for allowing me to share my own sacred river of Life—and for investing the time and care to get to know yours more intimately.

One natural culmination of sincere inner work is outer transformation. It is my hope that by traversing *The Real You*, you now have an enhanced capability to make a significant leap forward in contributing to the lives of others.

There has been a steady stream of transformational events on the planet over the past 2 decades: the horrific terrorist events that unfolded on the morning of 9/11; Barack Obama's historic election and his serving 2 terms as President of the United States; the international financial meltdown in 2008; a sea-change in perceptions in support of equal rights for the LGTBQ community sweeping the globe; the emergence of the #metoo women's movement.

The unspeakable cruelty of George Floyd's death, captured on video and shared with billions worldwide, ignited a radical shift towards addressing multi-generational racism and social injustice. His tragic and gruesome murder reached into people's sense of shared humanity, into our authentic nature that resides well beyond racial identity. This coincided with the worldwide COVID pandemic, followed by the Russia/Ukraine crisis that reflects the polarizing themes of democracy and authoritarianism, all providing an unprecedented opportunity for inner reflection and a radical reevaluation of societal priorities in communities around the globe.

"We cannot solve our problems with the same thinking we used when we created them."

~ Albert Einstein

I remember a powerful story from the mid-1960's that took place in a conservative, Bible-centered small town in Oklahoma. At the time, the gay and lesbian community in the town had made the decision to hold their first public gay pride event—a colorful parade down Main Street. When the townspeople heard this news, many of them were disturbed. Letters were written to the newspaper and violence was threatened. As the day of the parade approached, the organizers sought the counsel of the head monk at the monastery in the foothills outside of town. They asked if he would be willing to walk at the front, leading the parade. They shared with him that it was their hope that his presence might soften the spirit of hostility toward them. He graciously agreed, saying he would be honored.

When the parade began, Main Street was filled with townspeople. Indeed, they were shocked by the participation of the monk who, despite the palpable feeling of hatred in the air, gently strode forward, his face beaming with the presence of peace. Surprisingly, no violence or even verbal attacks ensued during the entire parade. A local newspaper reporter interviewed the monk afterwards, and inquired, "How were you able to maintain such equanimity in the face of the townspeople's fear and animosity?" He replied, "I learned years ago that the very best opportunity for moving deeper into my peace is in the presence of non-peace."

If we are to truly accept and honor people who live and act differently from us, a shift which is fundamental to our survival as a species, we must strengthen our ability to embrace all aspects of our inner world—our own inner diversity. Tending to our own sorrow and brokenness is part of the work of tending to the brokenness outside of us. When we can accept ourselves fully, we can more easily accept the strengths and weaknesses in other people. This solid ground of empathy and inclusivity is the cornerstone of a more awakened civilization.

Perhaps now more than ever before, we have a phenomenal opportunity to create a more just and honorable world. Some may be called to join in public demonstrations, others may choose to teach and inspire people, and still others may be drawn to raise their children with greater love and encouragement. Independent of the specific outer form, authentic leadership can make an enduring contribution to everyday lives in countless ways. No matter the size or nature of our respective contributions, each of us can step into an integral role in this larger movement. Hope lies in acknowledging what we are capable of, and while Spirit paves the way, it is up to each of us to respond to our inner calling to contribute.

"The spiritual journey is a creative journey. It's about birth. It calls us past the boundaries of convention. It tests our willingness to see life in a new way—and our courage to express it."

~ Anne Hillman

Part of my calling has been to write the book you hold in your hands. It's been germinating in my heart for close to 2 decades, and I finally summoned the courage and discipline to step forward. With the untold support of so many, I stand here marveling that it has finally been completed.

One of the unexpected blessings of the book's unfolding is the way it has served as a healing balm for my family. Prior to publication, I sent my ex-wife, Susan, a draft of the passages in the book that involved her. Given the traumatic nature of how our marriage ended and the fact that we hadn't been in intimate communication for a few years, I felt trepidation that she would be triggered and upset with me. Thankfully, she was deeply moved by the many ways I honored her, and she acknowledged me for daring to express myself so vulnerably throughout the book. This sharing bridged a painful distance between us and brought us closer.

After sending a draft of the manuscript to my estranged son Christian, he shared with me how moved he was by what I'd written. He expressed his sincere thanks for the tools in the book, as he is finding them immensely helpful on his journey of recovery. The book also provided me and my older son Johnny with the opportunity for many tender and healing conversations about the painful experiences we had traversed together in our family.

I also shared key passages of the book with my sister Cathy. She was moved by what I wrote about her, and relayed some new details about our brother Michael's heroic life after prison that I was able to include in the book.

She confided to me that a few years back she had entered therapy for the first time to address an underlying sense of unworthiness and depression. In the process, she unearthed a pivotal traumatic memory that had taken place for her in junior high school and which precipitated her choosing into a life of drugs. In the girls bathroom one day, she had begun comparing herself to other girls and had come to the conclusion that she was unattractive and not lovable. With the therapist's support, she connected with her Authentic Self and, in her imagination, re-entered that pivotal scene and lovingly embraced her little girl, letting her know she was indeed quite beautiful and lovable. After this passage of healing work, the trauma and accompanying depression she had been carrying for over 50 years began to steadily lift. I asked her if I might include her story in the book, and she said, "Of course, that's what the book is all about. My story may help someone else on their journey."

All living things are individual instruments through which the Spirit of Life reveals itself. What secret projects reside in your heart? How might you courageously bring them forward to transform the landscape of your life in ways that expand the limits of your imagination? When you pursue your dreams and don't hold back, you make unforeseen breakthroughs. I predict that you, too, will stand and marvel at the projects and contribution you dare to bring forward in this life.

Ecologist Suzanne Simard has pioneered research into the secret life of trees and what she refers to as "forest wisdom." She has discovered that trees employ an elaborate, interconnected network of buried soil fungi to communicate their needs to each other. They share timely warning signals about environmental changes, and collaborate in the transfer of available nutrients among neighboring trees to sustain life for their whole ecosystem.

In a similar way, everyone on the planet lives in an interdependent relationship with everyone else. All Authentic Selves are connected. Each of us has an opportunity to nourish our inner roots so that they run more deeply into the ground and connect us more vibrantly with others. By reading this book, you have further activated your root system.

Our planet is getting increasingly smaller. As the human population continues to climb, as climate change accelerates environmental disruption, and as globalization and technology increasingly connects all human beings with one another, we have created a fertile environment for joining together and collaborating as a planetary family.

You've made it this far by engaging in the real work involved in deepening your Self-knowledge. As a completion ceremony, I invite you to place your hands upon your *Authentic Self Journal* and bless all the experiences of healing and revelation that have been captured within its pages.

Yes, we are Divine, but we are also remarkably human. We are designed to live authentically, and the key is to bow to our unique design just as it is. I extend my heartfelt blessings to your beloved Authentic Self. May its strong and tender glow unite with that of others to reach every unlit place on this planet.

A GLORIOUS CONSPIRACY

by Gavin Frye

This life has been full, well
beyond my youthful imaginations.
I carry a stillness,
immersed in the buoyant water
that surrounds and blesses
this boat called Home.

Whole and content, this presence
says, "All we've created and
experienced in this life has been plenty."
Yet, the longing to live ever-more
generously burns inside.

How does a smoldering fire
relight itself without hands
when it knows there's a secret reserve
of warmth hidden in its core?

May I be blessed with
the courage to flow in new
currents of unbridled generosity,
to express in prolific ways the
sacred orchestration of gifts
flowing through this vessel,
to be used-to-tatters in the
days and years that remain.

ABOUT GAVIN

PROFESSIONAL BACKGROUND & EXPERIENCE

Graduate Degrees

MA in Counseling & Guidance from California State University Northridge

MA in Spiritual Psychology from the University of Santa Monica in California

Professional Experience

In private practice as a licensed Marriage and Family Therapist in California since 1983.

Served on faculty for 16 years at the University of Santa Monica from 1987-2002, co-facilitating the Masters Degree program in Spiritual Psychology.

Designed and facilitated transformational workshops, including:

- ❖ THE REAL YOU: Leading Your Life From Your Authentic Self, an online workshop series built around the key themes from the book (20 sessions)
- ❖ AUTHENTIC SELF LEADERSHIP: Birthing the Next Season of Your Life's Expression (11 months)
- ❖ SOUL-CENTERED PARENTING: Guiding Your Family from the Wisdom of the Heart (12 weeks)
- ❖ TURNING POINT: Discovering & Creating Your Life's Work (4 days)

PERSONAL

After spending the majority of my life in Southern California and raising three beautiful children, over the last six years I've been blessed to have relocated to the Pacific Northwest. I live in a beautiful waterfront home on Lake Stevens, 30 miles north of Seattle.

I am continually immersed in discovering new body-centered, psychological and spiritual modalities that support evolving to new levels of healing and awakening. I have many passions, including: international travel, celebrating a wide range of music and dance from around the world, peaceful kayak outings on alpine lakes, and daily partaking of the healing presence and beauty of nature.

ADDITIONAL OFFERINGS FROM GAVIN

❖ THE REAL YOU

Adventures in Authenticity

~ Online Support Community ~

"Would you like to know about a dynamic online program held over time that builds upon your experiences with this book? That could assist you in cultivating a deeper connection with the presence and wisdom of your Authentic Self? I warmly invite you to join me from the comfort of your own home for these healing, empowering and cost-effective live video gatherings which are centered around the core teachings and exercises in this book—and much more!

This regularly scheduled workshop series, which you can start at anytime, provides the knowledge, support and guidance you need to deepen your connection with the unique energies of your deeper nature. It is for anyone seeking ways to sustain their personal integrity and courage amidst the challenges of our time. You'll be joining an intimate and affirming community of fellow travelers from all around the world, each pursuing their own hero's journey of healing and awakening.

Each online gathering is designed as a learning sanctuary, a safe space for authentic sharing and inspired discovery. Within each session, I will be leading an in-depth exploration of core principles from the book along with personal life stories; leading the group in a hands-on exercise designed to invite a flow of inner revelation; and facilitating a few brief one-on-one mentoring sessions with selected group members.

Group members will also have the opportunity to build rich, ongoing connections with fellow participants, a golden resource that naturally flows within a safe, sacred community. This series provides an ongoing, soulful forum for rich dialogue where we can support each other as we engage in the journey of "Leading Your Life From Your Authentic Self."

I invite you to visit my website at gavinfrye.com where you'll find all the detailed information you'll need to participate in these heartfelt and adventurous online gatherings. I look forward to seeing you there!"

You can learn more about the following services by visiting my website at gavinfrye.com:

- ❖ ONE-ON-ONE MENTORING
- ❖ COUPLES MENTORING
- ❖ KEYNOTE SPEAKING & CONFERENCE ENGAGEMENTS
- ❖ MASTERMIND PROGRAMS

SOCIAL MEDIA

- Instagram: @gavinjamesfrye
- Linked In: @gavin-frye
- TikTok: @gavin.frye
- Youtube: @Gavin Frye
- Meta: @GavinFrye.8
- Facebook: gavin.frye.98

ACKNOWLEDGEMENTS

I've discovered firsthand that it indeed takes a devoted village to birth our highest aspirations in this world. So many gracious and generous Souls have blessed me and this project with their loving collaboration and signature gifts:

❖ Each member of my family, who've provided extraordinary love and delivered essential life lessons on my path of healing and awakening.

❖ John-Roger and John Morton, two of my primary teachers in this lifetime. For over four decades, they have inspired me with their steady demonstration of Spirit-led living.

❖ Carl Jung, whose profound dedication and courage has birthed glimpses into the life of the soul like no other. His unique signature has infused my heart with depth and revelation for decades.

❖ James Mihaley, my exquisite best friend and beloved editor—and the most gifted creative partner I have ever known. His talent, which he delivers so consistently and generously, is divine inspiration.

❖ David Whyte, the quintessential poet of the heart, who has gifted me for decades with his profound wisdom and eloquence in capturing the intimate journey of the soul.

❖ Ron & Mary Hulnick, who blessed me in immeasurable ways during my 16-year apprenticeship at the University of Santa Monica—with their devoted leadership at the helm.

❖ Candace Wheeler, my life-long golden friend who intuitively knew, 40 years ago when we first met, all that I was destined for in this lifetime. You've been a shining north star.

❖ Rita Rivera Fox, my joyful mentor and Anam Cara, who consistently and joyfully ushers me into an ever-expanding, flourishing life.

❖ Virginia Farrington, my beloved soul sister over many decades who also blesses me with her website design talents and playful inspiration.

❖ Amma Li Grace, a dedicated fellow traveler who has taught me so much about how to trust and embody the divine feminine.

❖ Patrice Kahn, who has offered me friendship and devotion of the highest caliber for years.

❖ James Price, a brilliant prince of a friend who has been there for me during the most challenging times of my life.

❖ Alexander Tolken, a modern day mystic and supremely gifted astrologer who steadily shines divine wisdom on my path.

❖ Nathaniel Solace, a steadfast and loving friend who also gifted me with the initial visual design of my front book cover.

❖ Scott Oldford & Libby Crow, soulful and generous friends who've I've been privileged to have by my side for many years.

❖ Mel Stach, a true friend of the heart who enriches my life each and every time we connect.

❖ George Kao, a genius wayshower in the fine art and craft of stewarding an authentic, heart-centered business.

❖ Oshri Hakak, who provided invaluable wisdom and playfulness as we collaborated in the final editing and publishing of this work.

❖ Hillary Barker, a multi-talented graphic designer who provided top-notch collaboration on every aspect of designing the book cover and interior design.

❖ Laurel Airica, who provided loving, seasoned editing of the first draft of my manuscript.

❖ Chelsea Didier, Seth Kadish, Michelle Rogers, Rachel Bell, Sam Shaw, Melyssa Griffin, Amanda Bucci, Craig Clemens and Miriam Orque—all heartfelt friends who continue to inspire and support me with their remarkable love and entrepreneurial talents.

Lightning Source UK Ltd.
Milton Keynes UK
UKHW050443211122
412554UK00010B/623